An Actor's Odyssey

ORSON WELLES TO LUCKY THE LEPRECHAUN

BY **ARTHUR ANDERSON**

FOREWORD BY **ANNE MEARA**

AN ACTOR'S ODYSSEY:
ORSON WELLES TO LUCKY THE LEPRECHAUN
©2010 ARTHUR ANDERSON

Published in the USA by:

BEARMANOR MEDIA
P.O. BOX 71426
ALBANY, GEORGIA 31708
www.BearManorMedia.com

ISBN-10: 1-59393-522-1 (alk. paper)
ISBN-13: 978-1-59393-522-6 (alk. paper)

FRONT COVER: ON *TONY AND GUS* — 1935

BOOK DESIGN AND LAYOUT BY VALERIE THOMPSON

PREFACE

A publisher's representative recently gave a sure-fire formula for the success of any book. Book-signing tours and cocktail parties for critics were becoming passé, he said. They were too expensive and no longer that effective. Any book would almost sell itself, he added, as long as it was based on one of these subjects:

SEX

GOD

DOGS

ABRAHAM LINCOLN

Though this one will at least touch on the first three, I have not yet figured on how to bring in our 16th President.

It is the story of a little boy — me — who lived a rich theatrical life on suburban stages, minor radio stations and in his own imagination, then became a professional actor at the age of twelve. As of now my career has not completely subsided, but let the first 72 years suffice.

There is a certain fascination attached to anyone who has the guts — or the gall — to deliberately get up on a stage or in front of a camera and pretend to be someone else, and to apparently enjoy it. Though Arthur Anderson will never be a household name, I can claim to have been performing professionally since 1935, making a living — sometimes a very good one — and in that time I've had some joyful experiences, some depressing ones, and have worked with many fascinating people — and a few rotters. But in their own way they were fascinating, too.

ACKNOWLEDGMENTS

I like to think I wrote this book by myself, but in theatrical terms it would have closed out of town without the valued help of many people. Good friend Craig Wichman was first, with essential factual research. Ideas and information I gratefully received from Edgar Farr Russell III, as well as from Derek Tague and Stanley J. Weinberg, Ph.D. I have also been initiated into the mysteries of the computer thanks to Bernadette Fiorella, Magie Dominic, and friend and neighbor Bob Bettendorf.

The lively Foreword by Anne Meara has provided a warm sendoff, for which I am truly grateful.

My wife Alice has worked with me throughout, giving much useful criticism, theatrical advice and loving help.

TABLE OF CONTENTS

PREFACE . . . 1

ACKNOWLEDGMENTS . . . 2

FOREWORD BY ANNE MEARA . . . 3

CHAPTER ONE: A LIGHTHOUSE IN MY BACKYARD . . . 5

CHAPTER TWO: SMITTEN AT AGE FOUR . . . 11

CHAPTER THREE: MOVING TO MANHATTAN . . . 20

CHAPTER FOUR: ADVENTURES WITH ORSON . . . 33

CHAPTER FIVE: MORE OF THE MERCURY . . . 50

CHAPTER SIX: STAGE AND RADIO IN MY TEENS . . . 55

CHAPTER SEVEN: INTO THE WILD BLUE YONDER . . . 72

CHAPTER EIGHT: LOOKING FOR WORK . . . 89

CHAPTER NINE: FINDING WORK . . . 100

CHAPTER TEN: BIKING THROUGH EUROPE, FINDING MY ROOTS . . . 111

CHAPTER ELEVEN: EIGHT YEARS A BACHELOR . . . 119

CHAPTER TWELVE: MY LIFE AS A LEPRECHAUN . . . 144

CHAPTER THIRTEEN: 87 PERRY STREET . . . 155

CHAPTER FOURTEEN: BACK FROM CHICAGO . . . 177

CHAPTER FIFTEEN: RE-ENTER ORSON WELLES . . . 198

CHAPTER SIXTEEN: WINDING DOWN . . . 202

OTHER WRITINGS BY ARTHUR ANDERSON . . . 201

INDEX . . . 210

Gratefully Dedicated

To The Memory of

David Belasco Howard

FOREWORD

BY ANNE MEARA

Cream of Wheat is so good to eat, yes, we have it ev'ry day,
We sing this song, it will make us strong, and it makes us shout
"Hooray!" It's good for growing babies and grownups too to eat,
For all the fam'ly's breakfast, you can't beat Cream of Wheat.

ANNOUNCER: *Cream of Wheat, the great American family cereal*
presents Let's Pretend!

This was the sponsor for *Let's Pretend*, the popular radio show from the '30s and '40s, and I was a superfan. I couldn't wait to turn on the radio every Saturday morning and hear Sybil Trent, Gwen Davies, Miriam Wolfe, Arthur Anderson and cast do *Jack and the Beanstalk, Cinderella, Sleeping Beauty* and *Rumpelstiltskin.* I wanted to do that, too. Forever branded in my memory is the famous baby cry of Sybil Trent, and all the wonderful voices of my favorite childhood characters.

My husband Jerry and I met while "Making the Rounds," which is what an actor did in "those days" to be seen by an agent. Arthur was also in those offices; we might have passed each other in the hallway and I didn't even know it. And even though Jerry and I never worked with Arthur, our paths had similar stories: working in radio and commercials, Broadway and off-Broadway. Arthur just got started a little earlier. He was lucky enough to be a child radio star.

I didn't meet Arthur Anderson until much later, when I had the pleasure of partaking in a panel at The Museum of Broadcasting, honoring a reunion of the cast of *Let's Pretend*. I was lucky enough to become friends of Sybil Trent and Miriam Wolfe, the artists behind the voices, who I had listened to at an early age. And as I learned of Arthur's upbringing and life as a "working" actor, I realized that all of us, whether we are a household name or not, share a common bond, the love of the work and the joy of always working. Arthur Anderson certainly proved that he was never going to live the life of a "starving actor."

Actors today have the Internet as their audition tool; they can text, e-mail, blog, YouTube, Facebook, iChat and Skytype. But Arthur Anderson had a career before cell phones; a time when you slid the resume under the door and called the message center to see if you had gotten a callback. As *An Actor's Odyssey* shows, it's still about being an actor: about the words, the work and the cast that becomes a family, at least until the show is over.

Arthur Anderson has many years of shows, commercials and voices that he shares with us in this, and he includes wonderful memories about meeting his wife, the birth of their daughter and his time in the Army as a young man. The streets of an actor living and working in New York come alive. Enjoy the tour.

1
CHAPTER
A LIGHTHOUSE
IN MY BACKYARD

Every year scores of young actors from all parts of the United States stream into New York City, hoping to begin successful careers. I am one of a minority. I was born there.

It was a long trip to Edinboro Road, Richmond, Staten Island . . . from Copenhagen, Denmark, where my father was born . . . as long as it was from *Leasom*, a grand house on a hill in Sussex, England, my mother's birthplace, overlooking "The Ancient Town Of Rye."

My father lost his father when he was a year old. His mother eked out a living partly by pickling pigs' feet given to her by a slaughter house, and selling them to sailors off the ships. Somehow, George Christian Andersen was able to get an education, and after graduating from engineering school in Copenhagen he emigrated to the United States in 1907. There an immigration officer misspelled his name, changing it from the Danish "Ander**sen**" to the incorrect Swedish "Ander**son**," and rather than make trouble my father let it stand. He first worked with his brother Albert at the General Electric Company in Schenectady, New York, then he got a job with the Stone & Webster engineering firm, principally building electric power plants. One of them was at a copper mine in Guymas, Mexico, which could only be reached by a train that ran once a week. A later assignment was in Savannah, Georgia, and that was where he met my mother.

Violet Elizabeth Brookfield was one of the six children — four daughters and two sons — of Colonel Arthur Montagu Brookfield and the former Olive Hamilton, she of Buffalo, New York. After retiring from the British Army and serving in Parliament for eight

The Lighthouse.

482 Edinboro Road.

years, he became a British Consul, an officer of the government who promoted trade with foreign countries.

The Colonel was assigned to the Free City of Danzig, Germany, where my mother, the most spirited of the Brookfield daughters, was courted by a young German naval officer who proposed marriage to her. For some reason she turned him down, and the young man was crushed and heartbroken.

My grandfather was then sent to the consulate in Savannah, Georgia. A power plant was being constructed there and George Anderson was assigned to show the Consul's daughter around. It had rained the night before, and holding her hand to guide her over the mud puddles he fell instantly in love with Violet Elizabeth Brookfield. My mother, stricken with guilt at what she had done to the young officer, had determined, possibly to atone for her sin, that she would marry the next man who asked her. She and my father were married at St. Paul's Church in Savannah, August 7, 1914.

I was the youngest of the three Anderson boys; Edward Christian, born in Boston, in 1917, George Cecil, born in Brooklyn, in 1919, and Arthur John Miles, born on Staten Island, on August 29, 1922. My parents had explored Staten Island and found there an eight-room stone house with two chimneys and casement windows in Richmond at 482 Edinboro Road on Lighthouse Hill, within sight of the Ambrose Channel Light, a Staten Island landmark. The house reminded my mother of an English manor house.

Our house was isolated. It was near the end of Edinboro Road, a dirt road just before you came to the LaTourette Golf Course, which we called *The Links*. The way up from the village of Richmond below was by *The Steps* — 106 stone steps, which were beautiful, and shaded by spruce trees which gave forth a wonderful, mysterious whispering sound when the wind was up.

The inconvenience of not having a car was offset by a woman named Alice and her grown children, Georgia and Launie. They were an African-American family sent by my grandfather, and they lived in a little one-room house between the garage and the chicken house. Alice was my nursemaid, and one of my earliest and happiest memories is sitting on her lap in their doorway, eating buttered rice which she fed me from a bowl. My mother, having been brought up in large houses with servants, was no doubt happy to have this continued on the hill at Richmond. Parenthetical note: Their surname was never told me and I never thought to ask.

My nickname was Tokey ("Watch out for his little tokums"). I was loved and cosseted by my parents and by Alice and her family, if not particularly by my brothers. When I was brought home from the hospital, my brother George said, "Take it away!"

There were not many families on Edinboro Road, and people with boys seemed to move in and out with great regularity. One family that stayed, though, were the Heffernans. They lived in the two-family yellow-brick house next to the lighthouse. Two lighthouse keepers had lived there in the days when the light was fed by kerosene.

Johnny Heffernan and I got along well, and confided in each other. I remember the day when he came with the news that he had heard it felt good to put your thing in a girl's place, the nomenclature at our ages not being very precise. And I wondered, *Why would anyone want to do a thing like that?*

The lighthouse and the lighthouse keeper's house were built of light yellow brick.

The whole complex, built by the Government, was quite impressive, and that included the landscaping. In front of the house were three grass terraces, and at least once Johnny and I rolled down all three in one motion. I do not remember my mother's reaction to the state of my clothes after that, but it couldn't have been favorable. Later, I had a much grander adventure. I happened one day to find the lighthouse unlocked. Men were at the top, probably polishing the light's huge reflectors. I climbed the iron stairs inside. It was a clear spring day and from the top I could see the Ambrose Channel to the south, where ocean liners came in, and westward to the end of the Island, all the way to Tottenville and Raritan Bay. It was not until I moved into Manhattan that I fully realized that Staten Island, then a series of small villages at the southern tip of New York State, was part of one of the largest cities in the world.

Our house had been built in 1911 by a Frenchman named D'Autremond. A large, empty, old-fashioned, round-topped trunk was in the attic with his name painted on it. My father bought the house in 1920 from Louis Bergman, who, it was said, had won it in a poker game. Privet hedges and a cedar rail fence surrounded the house. Below the south end of the property was a miniature fruit orchard, but it had not been tended in many years, and I found there only some wrinkled, stunted peaches. Other things that bespoke the well-to-do former owner included a pergola with a grape arbor behind the kitchen, and what we called the "glass house," built against the south wall, where plants and flowers were meant to be kept. My father did not have the time or the money to maintain the property as Mr. D'Autremond had done, but these various remnants of former affluence were a part of my childhood.

As you entered the front hallway through a Dutch door (built in two sections), you saw the staircase to the upper floors in front of you. On the right was the doorway to the dining room, which had a six-foot mirror on the wall, standing on a carved oak base. Its silvery backing had become mottled around the edges. On the left side of the hall through French doors was the living room, twelve-by-twelve feet. It had built-in oak bookcases with glass doors, and a brick fireplace with an ornately carved Italian cherry wood mantel. We had an upright piano which my mother played, but no radio until I started in school.

As the young girl Emily asks the Stage Manager in Thornton Wilder's *Our Town*, "Do any of us realize life as we live it?" I certainly did not in my young days on the Island. It is only looking back, after all these years, that I sometimes fall asleep bringing back the magical snapshots of my childhood — the house in Richmond — the woods — the ponds — the village — St. Andrew's Church — the smell of honeysuckle and of creosote on telephone poles — the sounds of crows and bluejays, and the wind in winter. All this, and having a lighthouse practically in my backyard.

2
CHAPTER
SMITTEN AT AGE FOUR

Though acting talent cannot be taught, it can be encouraged and developed. My first performance was at age four. One evening when there were guests, my mother lifted me up on a living room table to do a little song she had taught me. The guests all applauded. I distinctly remember saying, "Would you like me to do it again?" Their reply was no thank you, but that did not matter. I had had my first taste of audience reaction — and I was smitten.

There were many more opportunities during the following years on Staten Island. The first was at St. Andrew's Church, where there was a competition for the best recitation of The Lord's Prayer. It was decided that there was a tie, between me and the little boy whose mother was the donor of the winner's silver cup. Robert Lewis and I were to own it alternate months, but their big Nash kept getting stuck in the mud as they tried to turn around in front of our house to return it, and the Lewises decided that this was not worth it. I still have the cup, tarnished but intact.

Since my elder brothers Edward and George brought home language from the public school in Richmond that shocked my mother, she enrolled all three of us at St. Patrick's Catholic School, also in the village. The Andersons were the only Protestants there. The Sisters of St. Dorothy were devoted but strict. I remember having been rapped on the knuckles with a ruler more than once. I got a chance to perform at a graduation exercise in the new building on Clarke Avenue; I was given the part of a delivery boy for a shoemaker. When the other boys asked me to come and play, I piously waved my index finger left and right and sang, to the tune

At The Children's Playhouse.

of *London Bridge Is Falling Down*:

"No, I can-not go and play, go and play, go and play . . . ."

Thus, encouraging child labor. I knew it was hokey, but did as I was told.

In 1930 I finally got to perform on a real stage. It was at the Children's Playhouse, in a little barn in Dongan Hills, owned by former actress Cecyl Grimes, who later became a dear friend. I remembered having seen her child actors doing *The Pied Piper of Hamelin.* The town was infested with rats, and there were a dozen children scampering on stage in rat costumes. I distinctly remember thinking, "That looks like fun. I'd like to do that." My first role at the Playhouse, at age eight, was Rip Van Winkle in a Christmas pageant, *How Santa Claus Was Saved for Christmas.* To quote from *The Staten Island Advance*:

> "Rip Van Winkle was skillfully portrayed by Arthur Anderson, who acquired for the occasion a sturdy Dutch accent. He won great applause for his song to his dog Schneider." I was in heaven.

When I was about ten, Miss Cecyl introduced me to Malcolm Beggs, a New York actor who was doing a one-week engagement of *Rip Van Winkle* at the Park Theater on Targee Street in Stapleton. I was one of the children, and probably had a couple of lines; I waited for my cues in the wings, stage left. I had never been backstage in a real theater before. It seemed enormous, and it was magic, because as you looked up at the flies, they went on and on into the darkness.

I admired the way Rip Van Winkle's awakening from his 20 years' sleep was handled. While Mr. Beggs Senior, as old Rip, stretched and yawned, his son Malcolm Lee, who was young Rip in the first act, was playing *Morning* from Greig's *Per Gynt Suite* on a windup phonograph. When it was time for the music to fade down, pudgy young Beggs simply closed the phonograph's cover, and sat on it.

I also got to play in an amateur hour at the Paramount Theater on Bay Street, a recently-built orange-brick art-deco gem. Besides pictures it also featured *Betty and Jean at the Twin Organs* — Wurlitzer, of course. They both smiled at the audience and played the latest hits — but there was a gimmick. One of the keyboards was a dummy.

In 1933 the Children's Playhouse took part in a huge pageant at the Paramount, *The Romance of Books.* One of the acts was a playlet,

The Prince Who Learned Everything Out of Books. He thought that everyday humans were characters from fairy tales. I was Tony, his long-suffering page. The whole show was much too long, and our sketch was cut from the second performance.

Cecyl Grimes at the Playhouse was assisted by Charles Kenny, brother of the well-known songwriter Nick Kenny. They co-authored the big hit songs *Love Letters in The Sand, There's A Gold Mine In The Sky,* and many others. Kay, as we called him, also wrote songs independently of his brother, of a more fanciful nature. Some of his titles were *I'm Planting Little Onions So I Can Cry Over You,* and *Ev'ry Street Is Canal Street In Venice.* Kay wrote music for our stage plays and also radio scripts, which we did on Station WHN. (Take the elevator to the top of Loew's State Theater building and walk up one flight.)

Doing radio there was a challenge, because there was only one studio and the program before ours was a jazz combo. About two minutes before the end of their last number, the saxophonist stopped playing, put his instrument in its case and walked out. Then another instrument stopped, and another, and the show ended with only two musicians playing. While the announcer closed their show and introduced ours, the musicians slid out of the studio and we children tiptoed in. It worked very well. One other WHN memory was playing Scrooge at the age of eleven in a modernized version of *A Christmas Carol,* written by Kay.

Once recalled, other memories of my childhood in radio come flooding back. In 1933 I was on *Nick Kenny's Radio Kindergarten.* It was MC'd by Kay's better-known songwriting brother. He was also a columnist for the *Daily Mirror* — three cents daily, with an early sports edition for two cents. The show was on WMCA, 570 — At the Top of Your Dial. The performers on the one-hour program on Sundays were all children, with Marie Keefe at the piano. There was Eddie Grady playing his drums (monotonously), Mary Small singing (she later became a pop singing star), and Margaret McClaren, soprano. Baby Jean Lee, no more than six, did monologues written by her father, filled with corny gags. One was "Gee, I'm glad I don't like spinach, because if I liked it I'd eat it, and I hate the darn stuff." I did little two-minute sketches written by my mother and me, in which I did all the voices, and occasional dog barks. I remember being introduced by Nick thus: "And now here is that little menace from Staten Island."

In 1935 an *almost*-radio performance was on *The Ray Perkins Amateur Hour* on CBS, sponsored by Feen-A-Mint chewing gum laxative. The winners were decided by audience applause. I auditioned doing my hick sketch: an old New England farmer, and was told I'd be on the show that night. As we walked up Eighth Avenue, my mother was singing, *Tokey's on the Feen-A-Mint Hour, Tokey's on the Feen-A-Mint Hour* . . . . When we returned for the broadcast, I was told I wouldn't be on. Having a cute kid was unfair competition, the producers decided, and I'd be sure to win the prize.

The summer of 1935 was the start of a huge change in my life. We were being visited by an old friend of my mother's from Savannah, Nellie Abrahams. While in New York she saw another old friend of hers, George Frame Brown. He was an actor and writer, then having a great success on the NBC Blue Network with *Tony and Gus*, a five-a-week lighthearted show about Tony, an Italian immigrant (the singer Mario Chamlee), and his friend Gus (Brown), a Swedish prizefighter. Mr. Chamlee had two songs in each show, accompanied by a small orchestra led by Josef Stopak, with the accordion of Charles Magnante. It was sponsored by Post Toasties Cereal. They needed a little boy in the show, and Nellie recommended me. I auditioned for Mr. Brown in a Manhattan hospital where he was recovering from hernia surgery.

I was to be Buddy, an orphan who Tony and Gus meet in Cincinnati. Better still, when it was found that I could sing and play the ukulele, I got to do a couple of songs on one show. Friday, August 5, was my first performance, and I did a total of ten shows. The pay was fifteen dollars a show, totaling $150. This was three-and-a-half weeks before my 13th birthday, so I can still claim to have started my professional career at a cute age. The announcer was Edmund Ruffner, called Tiny because he was over six feet tall. It was he who uttered the first radio blooper I encountered. Doing a commercial for Post Toasties, he intoned: "Friends: do you wake up in the morning feeling dull, logy and lustless?"

My mother and I spent my two weeks' run in Manhattan living in a borrowed apartment at London Terrace, then as now an upscale apartment house with its own swimming pool, on 23rd Street. To get to NBC we would take a cross-town trolley, then the 6th Avenue el to 50th Street.

Doing a network radio show was an adventure. The only untoward experience of those two weeks was one night when I got up to go to the bathroom. Then I went sleepily back to what I thought was our bedroom on Edinboro Road, but it was someone else's apartment. It was summer, and many people left their doors open for ventilation, air conditioning being almost unknown then. A woman's voice said in the dark, "Is that you, George?" I suppose I was as frightened as she was. I apologized the next morning.

Back home on Edinboro Road, I now had some money in the bank. My mother had opened a trust account for me at the Staten Island Savings Bank in Stapleton. She kept close track of my earnings and expenses. One thing I had wanted was a new bicycle, and we bought one at Sears Roebuck. It was tan and brown, and had a battery-operated horn. The other thing was Gus, a Boston terrier puppy. I had picked him from a litter we saw in someone's living room in Stapleton. None of the pups were registered or had shots, and so I suppose mine was sick when I got him. There were some joyful months of owning Gus, but he died in my arms as we were being driven back from the vet's in a neighbor's car. That night through my tears I expressed for the first time what all of us do sooner or later in our lives: *Why me?*

In September I was back at school at St. Patrick's. Then calls started to come in to DOngan Hills 6-0111J for radio shows in Manhattan. The casting people had apparently noticed me on *Tony and Gus.* An hour and a half was not too long a trip to NBC, but doing an evening network show meant a repeat broadcast for the West Coast three hours later, and a very late night trip up the steps on Richmond Hill.

Meanwhile, in November, the Works Progress Administration was at its height, making work and giving paychecks to people who could not find employment, of whom there were thousands. My mother enrolled me in a WPA project, *How to Act in Motion Pictures,* for children. The classes were in a Manhattan loft building on 45th Street. There was a camera there which I could tell even then was antiquated. There was no film, and no lights. We were allowed to look through the viewfinder, but there was nothing I remember

George and Violet Anderson.

that had anything to do with motion picture acting. Its chief benefit was to provide an income for the instructor — the kind of thing that was known as "boondoggling."

All of this must have been an epiphany for my mother. Little Arthur was obviously destined to be an actor. Their marriage was not a happy one. Their backgrounds were too disparate. My father was the soul of patience and good humor. My mother told me that once when she came out with the frequent wifely complaint of "You don't love me — you don't care at all, etc.," his quiet reply was, "I like to hear you walking about."

Dad now worked for The Mack Truck Company in New Brunswick, New Jersey, a next-to-impossible commute. He kept a room there, and we only saw him twice a week. Alice and her family had been gone for several years. The coal stove on which they had cooked delicious meals was gone, too, and my mother had to use a kerosene stove, which stank, and stoke the coal furnace as well. She bitterly referred to our house as "the dump." Dad was warmhearted and kind, and a faithful husband who brought home a regular paycheck, but he was never a disciplinarian. Both my teenage brothers had their own problems. Edward was nervous and high-strung, and George was impossible for my mother to control, often getting into scrapes,

79 Greenwich Avenue.

the least of which was having an illegal motorcycle that she had taken away one day when he was at school. I am sure she felt fate had dealt her a bitter blow.

Violet Anderson was not the proverbial stage mother, grasping and competing on her child's behalf. She was an English lady who would never stoop to such things, but I believe she was now desperate. In the winter of 1935 she came to Manhattan and found a two-room apartment, two flights up, above Nolte's Delicatessen at 79 Greenwich Avenue in Greenwich Village. The monthly rent was $37.50.

My mother called Mr. Mills, the milk man, who came to Edinboro Road on a bitterly cold night in January and helped us load some furniture on his truck. The three of us drove to Greenwich Avenue and somehow got it all up the two flights of stairs. Another load was later brought by Tom Buccheri, the grocer, in his truck.

My mother told me that she had given my father an ultimatum: "Arthur and I are moving to Manhattan. Are you coming?" Dad could not live alone in the stone house that he had come to love. In only one respect, though, his life was now simpler. He could commute every day to New Brunswick on the Pennsylvania Railroad.

The Anderson family was now uprooted — torn apart. In 1935 my brother Edward had married Lorraine Gale, and, being underage, they had eloped to Elkton, Maryland. They spent their honeymoon in our sunroom, then moved in with her mother in Jamaica, Long Island.

George was a different matter. He was graduated from Curtis High School, but with his disciplinary problems was not allowed to receive his diploma at the ceremony. At first he lived alone at 482 Edinboro Road. Then, William Hurd Lawrence, our neighbor on the hill, who was a fine artist, was allowed to live in our house with his family for two years, and George lived with them — a boarder in what had been his own home. George's second marriage, years later, was to the Lawrences' daughter Dorothy, and in a letter she told me that George felt his mother had gone off and left him — which she had.

They had what could be called an adversarial relationship, but at age 18 he still needed his mother. After Mom, Dad and I had moved he once quietly said to her, "You do have two other sons." It might be expected that George would feel resentment toward me, as I was at least indirectly the cause of the family breakup. However, Dorothy wrote, he felt very proud of having a brother who was an actor, and boasted of me to all of his friends.

My acting career, then, was launched by a family being fractured. All these events were drastic upheavals for the Andersons, but an adventure for 13-year-old me.

3
CHAPTER
MOVING TO MANHATTAN

In January 1936 I moved quickly, and happily, from playing in the fields of Staten Island to working in skyscraper radio studios in Manhattan. I often thought about Staten Island and our house on the hill at Richmond, and visited the Island many times, but never once thought of moving back there. My young life had completely changed, and I was now busy being a radio actor. After those spasmodic performances mentioned earlier, I was now a professional.

In spite of the glamorous world of radio, an immediate question was, where would I go to school? That was solved fairly soon when having lunch at the Kaufman-Bedrick drugstore in the RCA Building. On the adjoining stool sat Peter Donald, a fellow cast member of a radio show I was doing. He said, "Of course you must go to PCS." This was The Professional Children's School, for, as the name implies, children performing in show business, most of them actors at that time. My mother and I had never heard of it.

PCS was started in 1914 by Jean Greer, the daughter of an Episcopal bishop, who on a backstage visit to see her friend Ruth Chatterton in the current Broadway hit *Daddy Long Legs* saw some children in the wings playing poker — for money. She asked them where they went to school. The reply was, "Oh, we don't have time to go to school. We're in a show."

With a *Well, we'll see about that* determination and the help of well-to-do friends, she started PCS in borrowed space at The Rehearsal Club, a residence for aspiring young actresses, which was then on West 45th Street. By the time I started there it had graduated to two floors in a small office building at 1860 Broadway, at 61st Street. The curriculum was limited to English, French, mathematics, history and civics. The work was not easy, but the atmosphere was congenial and supportive.

The school day started at 10:00 AM and ended at 2:15 PM so that students could make their matinees. They could get passes from the office to go to auditions, and if absent would turn in their work in writing. I fitted in quickly, made friends there, and graduated from grammar school on May 27, 1936. My diploma was signed and presented by Alfred Lunt. The tuition at PCS was $100 a year.

My first radio shows after *Tony and Gus* are hard to document, as my mother had not yet started the careful bookkeeping she later did for me. I know that one I did at NBC was *Capt. Healy's Stamp Club*, which included dramatizations, and though I don't recall auditioning there I did many jobs at CBS, starting in March 1936. One was for Himan Brown on *News of Youth*, a junior version of *The March of Time*.

Tony and Gus, my first paid radio work, was in the brand-new NBC studios at Radio City, which opened in 1932. After I passed under the "NBC Studios" marquee on 50th Street, I'd go straight ahead to the bank of eight elevators, each with an operator. Elevators were not automated in those days, and the operators wore white gloves.

The National Broadcasting Company was owned by The Radio Corporation of America, General David Sarnoff, president. Its New York studios were in the 70-story RCA Building, and the RCA neon sign on the roof could be seen miles away.

There were eight radio studios on the third floor alone. The two largest, 3-A on the left and 3-B on the right, could hold full orchestras and audiences as well, and 3-B had its own pipe organ. I could walk down the long hall to any of the six other studios, and during my 18-year radio career I am sure I worked in every one of them. Doors and woodwork were painted a subdued dark green, and each studio had inner and outer doors, to keep out unwanted sounds. The larger studios had silent, remotely-controlled sliding sound-absorbent panels, which could make the studio or parts of it more live for musical shows, and less live for dramatic broadcasts.

NBC was very proud of its "floating" studios, called that because they were literally hung from above on cables and not connected to the building's frame, so that outside sounds could not penetrate.

Besides its passenger elevators, the building still has a freight elevator big enough for a truck. In the Golden Age of Radio musicians carrying their instruments were told to use the freight car to get to the studios. This caused trouble once when the world-renowned violinist Jascha Heifetz, on his way to rehearse with Arturo Toscanini and The NBC Symphony Orchestra, was refused admission to the passenger cars by one of the young uniformed NBC pages. "But I am Jascha Heifetz," he said. "I don't care if ya Rubinoff," said the boy. Rubinoff and His Magic Violin was one of the popular musicians who specialized in schmaltz.

The seven CBS studios were in a smaller, less spectacular building at 485 Madison Avenue, corner of 52nd Street, which could not hope to match the grandeur of the NBC layout. The building had not been designed with radio in mind, and so the architects had made compromises. Studios 3 and 5, for example, on the 21st floor, needed to be about 20 feet high, for better musical reverberation. This meant that Studio 1, the station's largest, above on the 22nd floor, was up a flight of ten steps. This was only a problem when a grand piano or a large sound-effects console had to be lugged up or down.

I have photographs of what the CBS studios looked like when they were new. The walls had murals of skyscrapers, and ships under full sail. The microphones had been hung from the ceilings — very impractical, as they could not be easily moved to suit the needs of each program.

When I first worked at CBS in 1936, the studios and lobbies had been completely re-decorated in art-deco style. The lobbies had curved walnut panels, and mirrors. But two things I found much nicer than NBC's more impressive plant: first, warmer and closer human contacts in the smaller spaces. The other, that I remember most clearly, was the spectacularly beautiful view of the New York eastern skyline and the boats on the East River I saw as I got off the elevators on the 22nd floor.

A New York radio actor if in demand could do four or five shows a day, as rehearsals were much shorter than in theater or TV. Actors frequently had to hustle from one studio to another, especially if there were a conflict between two engagements. There was a bit of folklore that if you had a job at NBC, Rockefeller Plaza at 50th Street, then another the next minute at CBS, Madison Avenue at 52nd Street, you could take a shortcut through St. Patrick's Cathedral, midway between the two, but that if you stopped to genuflect you'd be late for rehearsal.

Only at first did my mother accompany me and wait outside during rehearsals or broadcasts. I quickly got used to the subways, the els and the trolleys. But in many ways I was a complete innocent. For instance, I had never been exposed to profanity in Richmond, Staten Island, where I had heard nothing more shocking than "Aw, go sit on a tack."

My education started one day during a rehearsal of *News of Youth* at CBS. A page entered the studio and told Himan Brown, the director, that there was a man outside with a message to deliver. Hi's response was, "Tell him to stick it up his ass." Another occasion was a program audition which took place in a suite at The Park Central Hotel. A man named Dugan and his wife were trying to convince a sponsor to buy their radio program, *Robinson Crusoe Junior.* Junior O'Day and I, playing two children shipwrecked in a storm, read our lines for the sponsor in the bedroom, while Mr. Dugan's wife was in the bathroom, playing a sound-effects record of fierce gale winds.

A middle-aged woman, evidently a friend of the Dugans', sat in as well. Apparently she had had quite a bit to drink. One of the last to leave, she was to catch a train at Pennsylvania Station. "Don't you think you'd better . . . err . . . go places before you leave?" asked Mrs. Dugan. "Nonshensh," said the woman. "I'll do it 'n the conductorsh eye." The little boy from Lighthouse Hill was growing up.

One exciting program I was on was *Vanished Voices*, done in one of the theaters CBS leased for audience shows. Bennett Kilpack starred as a professor who had invented a machine that could bring back voices from long ago in history. The show I was on was about the two celebrated Roman friends, Damon and Pythias.

In February NBC auditioned *Peter Absolute*, the story of a little boy in the days of the Erie Canal in the early 1800s. I was cast as Peter. The parts I played in those days were frequently orphans, who usually cried, and the character's first line was often, "Gee,

Mister . . . ." Peter, however, did not cry. The town had placed him in a boarding school with a cruel headmaster (Julian Noa), and a kindly kitchen maid (Jeanette Nolan) helped him escape. Enter then a tragedian of the old school, Augustus Crabtree (Ray Collins), who took Peter on tour with his company on the Erie. In various episodes Peter was abused, beaten, even slugged and thrown into the canal. It was a half-hour show, unsponsored, broadcast on the Red Network on Sunday afternoons, and it had a warm, humorous Dickensian flavor.

Our first broadcast was Sunday, March 23. We did it in Studio 3-H, last one down the corridor on the right. On sponsored radio programs child actors got the same fees as grownups, but NBC paid its moppet thesps, as *Variety* called them, $7.50, this for playing the lead on a half-hour program on the entire Red Network.

The director was Tom Hutchinson, and the organist was Bill Meeder, who played the theme, *Fifteen Miles on the Erie Canal*, in street barrel organ style. Our review in *Variety* included the following:

> "Impression left by the first chapter of this serial is strong. In all departments — acting, writing and settings it registers a decided forte. But its commercial possibilities will have to await further development. David Howard, erstwhile CBS continuity man and now freelancing, scripted the story, doing an able job. *Peter Absolute* is less local in its Americana, and the model quite obviously has been Dickens. Material, solidly strung together without any injections of synthetic sentimentality, is pretty severe for a radio cast. Performers, however, turned in a better than good account of themselves. Especially true of Arthur Anderson, whose *Peter Absolute* role required the majority of the lines. *Kid did socko work.*"

That has always been my favorite review.

Peter Absolute lasted through the summer and into September. It was more than a cut above the fifteen-minute daytime serials I usually played in. It was a thrill to be able to use my talents to the fullest in a quality program, though, of course, at the time I had very little understanding of how lucky I was.

David Belasco Howard, the writer of the program, was named after the producer David Belasco. His father was personal physician, and later all-around assistant to that prolific producer of many Broadway hits. David as a child had often been present at rehearsals and openings, and very early on was absorbing the atmosphere of the theatre. He later continued the tradition by becoming a playwright. His play *The Hermit Heart* won a Rockefeller Award, but was never produced. Ironically, second prize went to Tennessee Williams.

David, age 25, was tall, had a shock of wavy brown hair, a hearty laugh, and usually carried a cigarette. Doing *Peter Absolute* each week I got to know him well and he developed a fatherly affection for me. Before many broadcasts had gone by he referred me to Nila Mack, writer, producer and director of the long-running children's program *Let's Pretend*, which on Saturday mornings did dramatized fairy tales on the CBS network. I was quickly accepted by Miss Mack, and, just entering my teens, became a regular on the program, which featured the works of the Grimm Brothers, Charles Perrault, Hans Christian Andersen, and others. The cast were all children, who Miss Mack felt could best convey the openness, innocence and simplicity she wanted. Audiences and critics agreed, and *Let's Pretend* won many awards and lasted almost 25 years on CBS.

A character man from the start, I was never the handsome prince; instead, I might be an old man, a wicked giant or an enchanted talking horse, and I found that I had a talent for doing a different voice for each character I played. I do not believe that what I or any of the Pretenders did was hokey or exaggerated. Miss Mack would not have allowed it. We were dealing in fantasy, but our director insisted that it be played honestly.

As at NBC child actors were not paid grownup rates. On *Let's Pretend* each of us got $3.50 for a coast-to-coast network program. This did not matter to me, as I was getting such satisfaction out of doing something so imaginative and well written. And it was David Howard who started me on my *Let's Pretend* journey that lasted 18 years.

In the summer of 1936 my parents and I went to our Staten Island house on weekends, camping there as it were. Meanwhile, I had started to explore many parts of Manhattan, which was a different world. I found that milk and many other things were still being delivered in horse-drawn wagons. Once on Christopher Street I saw a horse pulling a wagon delivering Fleischmann's vinegar, which was still being sold in bulk to grocery stores.

It was only in later years that I realized how old-fashioned Manhattan had been when I first lived there. For instance, except in midtown and on Wall Street, most of the buildings were three and four stories high, built before elevators, and most had been residential. The sidewalks had round steel plates which had originally covered coal chutes.

Having always been fascinated by trains, I found the subways a delight, especially the oldest cars still in service. The 42nd Street shuttle, for instance, used old cars with hand-operated end doors, but the middle doors were pneumatic — some of the first invented, no doubt — and when closing each middle door made a sound which I compared to what must have been the high-pitched wheezing of a sick moose.

There were four elevated lines; the Second Avenue el, the Third, Sixth and Ninth Avenue, all of which ended at South Ferry. The oldest wooden el cars, used in rush hours, I particularly loved. Each car had open ends, and gates which had to be operated manually, and so for a seven-car train there had to be six conductors.

In the late summer of 1936 things started happening for me in a completely new direction. David O. Selznick's Selznick International Pictures was planning a spectacular version of Mark Twain's *Tom Sawyer*, to be shot on location in Twain's home town of Hannibal, Missouri. Without benefit of agent I was given a screen test — three, in fact — two for the role of Tom and one as Huckleberry Finn. They were shot at Eastern Service Studios in Queens (now Kaufman Studios). Nothing was heard immediately, and I continued a fairly busy schedule of radio shows, including *Let's Pretend* and *Peter Absolute*. In September, though, *Peter* was cancelled with no notice to David Howard, and so no way for him to bring Peter's story to a logical conclusion. We did our last broadcast on Sunday, September 16.

In that month I auditioned for Sinclair Lewis for a WPA production of his play *It Can't Happen Here*, adapted from the novel, which was to open in October. I came home and told my mother that I had gotten a part, and was to be in the show. "No, you're not," she said. "You're going to Hollywood."

Selznick International Studios.

My mother and I left from Grand Central on September 25 for California, under a five-week option for, presumably, more screen tests and possibly Hollywood stardom. The contract called for a salary of $100 weekly for me and $100 for my mother. Countersigning for Selznick were John Hay (Jock) Whitney, one of the company's chief bankrollers, and Katherine Brown, its New York casting director. My vivid memories of Selznick's offices at 230 Park Avenue include the highly polished brass hardware, and the elevators, each of which had on its ceiling a painting of a blue sky with fleecy white clouds.

The trip itself, four days I believe, was also an adventure. Change trains in Chicago, and take a Checker cab to get to another station. My mother and I traveled in a drawing room, and Selznick had sent someone to meet us at Pasadena. We were taken to Culver City, the headquarters of Selznick International. Our room was at the Washington Hotel, an unimpressive white stucco building within walking distance of the studio's front gate. There was no ceiling lighting fixture — only a bare bulb. So my mother hung an umbrella from the ceiling, and it provided quite nice indirect lighting.

While in Hollywood I was not neglected while waiting to go to work. For one thing, California law required that I be tutored, and there was a young man who did that in a room in one of the studio buildings. The lessons were not up to the level of what I was studying at PCS, and it was rather boring.

My mother and I were also taken on a motor trip down to Santa Monica. Another time we explored Olivera Street, the wonderful tourist-y Mexican enclave in Los Angeles. We were also able to board one of the red Pacific Railway trolley cars that took us to Venice Beach. And I piloted a little electric motorboat in Westlake Park.

Another grand experience was being given a membership in the West Side Tennis Club, where my mother and I had a lovely lunch one day. But all this had nothing to do with acting in a picture for Selznick. At least I was allowed in the studio one day where they were filming a scene from *The Garden of Allah* with Charles Boyer and Marlene Dietrich, who, glamorously dressed of course, was getting off a train.

The time dragged on interminably, and finally, as the five weeks were drawing to a close, my mother and I were called into the office — not to see David Selznick, but one of his lesser executives, a Mr. Richards. He told us that there was a snag in the company's plan to film in Hannibal. Due to the weather it was now obvious that no outdoor shots could be done until next spring. Meanwhile, little Arthur was growing — becoming taller and more leggy, and in a few months would no longer be an appealing, childish Tom Sawyer — or a good investment for Selznick. So it was a train back home again, after an interesting but wasted stay in the film capital. And it was back to radio, back to PCS and back to *Let's Pretend*. I did not feel any failure in that. I was glad to be home again.

My life would have been very different if I had played Tom Sawyer and been on Selznick's star roster. I will always be glad that I did not grow up in the high-pressure world of filmdom. Also forgotten was my father. What would he have done alone at 79 Greenwich Avenue? I don't believe my mother thought much about that. Arthur's career came first.

Later that fall at age 13, but looking and sounding younger, I was cast as Tommy, another orphan who occasionally cried, in *Bambi*, which would have been described as a warm family situation comedy. It was heard every Friday night on the NBC Red Network, sponsored by Sanka Coffee, through the Young & Rubicam ad agency. It starred Helen Hayes, and was written by my friend and mentor, David Howard, who I am sure, wrote the part especially for me. It was about a struggling young actress, Bambi, and her husband Jarvis, who live in a third-floor walkup. The names of evening dramatic shows were hardly ever given in the newspapers. Our show and most of the others were simply listed as *Sketch*. The orchestra was conducted by Mark Warnow, Raymond Scott's brother.

Miss Hayes was then playing in *Victoria Regina* on Broadway, and since the broadcast was from 8:00 to 8:30 P.M., she would do the show in full costume and makeup. Harry Essex, her manager, always had a cab waiting on the 49th Street side of the RCA Building. She had a standing arrangement with the same driver for years. When her last scene in *Bambi* was over, Mr. Essex hustled her into a waiting elevator, into the cab, and she was at the Music Box Theater just in time for the 8:40 curtain, making her entrance in the opening scene as the young Queen, with Vincent Price, who played the Royal Consort Prince Albert.

Besides myself, other supporting players in *Bambi* included James Meighan as her husband, Charlie Cantor, who later played Finnegan on *Duffy's Tavern*, and Adelaide Klein. They were a lovable old Jewish couple who ran a nearby store, while Arlene Francis was an actress friend.

Miss Hayes was very nice to me and gave me two matinee tickets for Christmas. As a thank you I ordered flowers in a Greenwich Village shop, but they were never delivered. I think the storekeeper thought I was just an adoring fan, and only a child, so figured he'd just forget about the delivery.

The studios on the 3rd floor were two stories high. Above the control room was a soundproof room with theater seats, where sponsors and guests could see and hear the show, and smoke if they liked. This was the Clients' Booth. On the hallway end of the studio was another glassed-in booth where the public could watch. Everyone called it "the goldfish bowl." NBC-guided studio tours would continually file in and out during our afternoon rehearsals. The page who was the guide would probably say, "That's Helen

Hayes down there, playing the lead. She's the famous stage actress who is now appearing on Broadway." Since there was a repeat broadcast for the West Coast at 11:30 PM, I would go back to the apartment and take a nap, then sleepily return to the studio. In one script Bambi had asked Tommy to watch out the window for a dinner guest who was expected soon. The script page read thus:

SOUND: (WINDOW OPENS)

TOMMY: He'll be up in a minute, Miss Bambi. He's
                    coming right in through the door.

But the (sleepy I guess) reply I read was: "He'll be up in a minute, Miss Bambi. He's coming right in through the window." I had inadvertently read the sound cue as part of my line. After the show Pete Barnum the director said to me, not unkindly, "Well, Mr. Anderson. That was quite a *faux pas* you made." "Why — what did I say?" I, of course, was completely unaware that I'd said it.

The high spot of the show's run for me was a Christmas dinner hosted by Miss Hayes for all the cast in the Rainbow Grill. *Bambi* lasted only one season, but it was a marvelous experience. I had done ten shows, the last being March 18. The fee was $75 per broadcast.

By the following spring my parents and I had moved to 52 Bank Street, corner of West 4th, still in West Greenwich Village. We were on the second floor of an old red brick building. There was more room for all three of us, and it was still near the subways. Incidentally, I remember that when I came home by taxi after a late-night broadcast, the New York City traffic lights had gone off at 1:00 AM.

At the time some of my radio shows included *David Harum*, and 15-minute dramatic shows starring the former motion picture actress Irene Rich. They always carried commercials about how slim she was, and how she owed it all to Welch's Grape Juice.

I was now getting steady radio work. Some of it was in recorded programs, including one called *Way Down East*. That was done at World Broadcasting, which occupied the old NBC studios at 711 5th Avenue. I remembered having auditioned there in 1934 for

Madge Tucker, who was directing a children's program called *The Lady Next Door*. Arriving at the 13th floor as directed, I had found a sunny reception room with soft carpets, a friendly middle-aged hostess, and a canary singing in a cage. Now the carpet, the hostess and the canary were gone, of course, and the place had become rather shabby. It was depressing when I compared it to its former elegance.

I had my first television experience on April 26, 1937, at NBC, coincidentally in Studio 3-H, where I'd done *Peter Absolute*. With all the lights, cameras and equipment the room now seemed so small. It was where NBC put its first experimental video programs on the air. The play was a short piece by George S. Kaufman called *The Still Alarm*. I still have the script, which I found recently. Two old friends are sitting in a hotel room. The bellboy (that was me) knocks politely and tells them the hotel is on fire.

ED:	This hotel?
BELLBOY:	Yes, sir.
BOB:	Well . . . is it bad?
BELLBOY:	It looks pretty bad, sir.
ED:	You mean it's going to burn down?
BELLBOY:	We think so — yes sir.

The two men agree that the fire department should be notified, but Ed has a better idea.

ED:	(To THE BELLBOY): Ring through to the Chief and tell him that Ed Jameson told you to telephone him. (To BOB) We went to school together, you know.

The sketch continues in that vein as the fire gets worse and worse. At one point the firemen arrive and one of them asks BOB for a match to light his cigar.

BOB: (Searching in drawer): I thought there were some here . . .

FIREMAN: Oh, never mind. (HE leans out the window and emerges with the cigar lit.)

Mr. Kaufman's script note was this: *It is important that the entire play should be acted calmly and politely. Every line should be acted as though it was an invitation to a cup of tea.* The sketch ended with sirens and whistles getting louder and smoke getting thicker, as one of the firemen plays *Keep the Home Fires Burning* on his violin. We were in the studio four days for the twelve-minute sketch. My pay for this was $35.

That summer I had my first experience at camp. Camp Anchorage was on Trout Lake in the hills west of Lake George. It was eight weeks of swimming, boating and hiking, and being with many boys my own age, which was good, and one time Donald Bain, with whom I later worked on radio, arrived on his bicycle, making a sound like a klaxon horn. Very early the next morning he took us on a bird walk. We were told to be very quiet, and his whistles attracted birds which came almost close enough to touch. After camp it was back to New York, to school and to my radio work. It was a time of growing, exploring and, joyfully, acting, which is when most actors will tell you they are most alive.

4
CHAPTER
ADVENTURES WITH ORSON

In May 1937 I auditioned at Professional Children's School and got the role of Gyp in *Second Hurricane*, which Aaron Copland called a "play opera." It was done for three performances at the Henry Street Playhouse on Grand Street, and directed by Orson Welles. The libretto was by Edwin Denby.

I had worked with Mr. Welles before, on *Peter Absolute*. He played Rex Dakolar, an English actor traveling with the Crabtrees, who was disdainful of all things American. He cared only for his spirit lamp and his little copper tea kettle. David had written another warm, funny Dickensian character, and young 22-year-old Orson, with his sonorous voice, played it to the hilt. Now only a year later he was to be my director. There were other PCS'ers in the cast: Buddy Mangan, Vivian Block and Estelle Levy (who later became Gwen Davies). Both of the girls were also Let's Pretenders. The three adult professionals in the cast included Joseph Cotten, who had the small role of an airplane pilot. The plot was that a hurricane and flood had devastated part of the country. Five young people volunteer to go and help. A second hurricane then hits, and they are marooned on a small island in the flood. A chorus of parents sat on bleachers on the stage. The orchestra was directed by young Lehman Engle. Copland's music was delightful and melodic, and very different from his more classical works. As Gyp I had a solo which included:

I wish I had a car, and just could drive away,
I wish I weren't so far, and didn't have to stay . . . .

One day during a lull in rehearsals my curiosity got the better of me and I explored the costume room in the upper reaches of the theater. Gwen tells me I then appeared on stage in an Abraham Lincoln tall hat, carrying an umbrella which had spokes but no cover.

We opened on Wednesday April 21, getting good reviews from all seven New York dailies. The only anomaly was that during rehearsals Orson Welles disappeared. He had gone to direct Marc Blitzstein's *The Cradle Will Rock* and his assistant Hiram Sherman took over the direction. There was a one-hour CBS network broadcast of *Second Hurricane* on Sunday May 9, directed by Earle McGill.

At this point David Howard entered my life again. He had known Orson from when he was a staff writer at CBS. He went to him to suggest that I play the role of Brutus' servant boy, Lucius, in the new Mercury Theatre's bare-stage production of Shakespeare's *Julius Caesar*. Orson, David says, was reluctant, but was finally convinced, and we began rehearsals on October 21 at the Comedy Theater at 108 West 41st Street, just west of Bryant Park.

The little theater was built in 1909 by the Shuberts, one of six that went up in New York that year, and it was their first foray north into the Times Square district. The theater's opening play was *The Melting Pot*, which reportedly kept audiences laughing for four months. The Comedy had a busy and illustrious history until March 1928, when *Maya*, a play about the life of a prostitute and the men who visit her on the quays of Marseilles, was shuttered by the New York District Attorney, who told both Lee Shubert and the cast that they would face fines and workhouse sentences if they failed to comply. Then, in 1929, the stock market crash caused the theater to go dark for two years. Its bookings were spotty after that, and in the summer of 1937 three shows opened and closed there in swift succession. In October its tenant was *Wall Street Scene*, billed as a comedy, which opened on the 18th and closed on the 20th after three performances, and the Comedy was dark again.

Orson and his partner, John Houseman, decided the building was just what they wanted. It had only 623 seats and two balconies, so no one in the audience would be very far from the stage. The house's very intimacy made Caesar's assassination, Brutus and Antony's orations and the lynching of the Cinna the poet more palpable and involving. The lobby was so tiny that an extension no more than six feet deep had been built over the sidewalk of 41st Street. In late October a new electric sign was hoisted on its roof in a ceremony supervised by press agent Henry Senber, and the theater became The Mercury. Ticket prices ranged from $2.20 for front row orchestra seats to 55 cents in the top balcony. It was to be truly a *People's Theatre.* This made little sense financially, for at those prices even if the Mercury sold out it could not make a profit. It was based on rosy optimism, and probably hot arguments between Orson Welles and John Houseman. The Mercury was capitalized for $9,000, much of it contributed by the poet Archibald MacLeish.

Rehearsals for *Caesar,* as our production was now called, were intense, to say the least, as Orson not only directed but also played Brutus. The only setting was a series of platforms, with a ramp sloping down toward the back of the stage. The brick wall was painted the color of dried blood, and I can still remember the smell of the fish glue which was used as sizer. The only thing resembling scenery was two huge flagpoles, one on each side of the stage. One day during rehearsal Joe Cotten was standing in front of the right flagpole, which had not yet been secured, and Orson told him, "Joe, if you don't watch out that thing is going to give you the goddamndest goose you ever got." The flag poles were later cut.

Mine was not a large part. My most memorable lines were the lyrics of a song which Lucius sings to Brutus in his tent the night before the Battle of Philippi. Shakespeare's direction reads only, "Music and a song." It was Orson's idea to borrow the lyrics from *Henry VIII,* another of Shakespeare's plays:

> "Orpheus with his lute, made trees and the mountain
> tops that freeze
> Bow their heads while he did sing, da dum dee
> dee dum . . ."

Shakespeare, of course, never wrote "Da dum dee dee dum." That was supplied by Marc Blitzstein, who wrote the melody and all the incidental music for *Caesar,* which was played by a small orchestra consisting of two brass instruments, Hammond organ and tympani.

I accompanied myself on a ukulele. It had a semi-circular mask attached, making it look like a lute. I called it my "lutelele." It was a Martin concert uke, with fuller tone than the ones young men used to serenade their girlfriends in the '20s. And since the song was a ballad it was played legato, not "plinkety-plink." I had bought it at Wurlitzer's, across the street from The Mercury. It cost fifteen dollars. I still have the uke, lovingly kept and sometimes played.

As rehearsals progressed Orson became somewhat waspish, but always in command, sure of what he wanted and how to get it from the cast, and had incredible energy and concentration. He became ill-tempered when things did not go well, and more than once was heard to scold other, older actors with, *Shame on you!* But the Mercury company all respected their 22-year-old director and tried to do their best in what promised to be an exciting production.

The temper tantrums were never directed at me. At age fifteen I was essentially still a child. One night when it was 2:00 AM and Actors' Equity overtime rules were being ignored, Orson noticed me yawning in one of the orchestra seats. "Go home, dear boy," he said. For all his moods he treated me with nothing but kindness. Though I refer to our director throughout as Orson, I never called him that. Children in the '30s were taught to respect their elders, so he was always Mr. Welles to me, even though there was only seven years' difference in our ages.

Orson was faultless at what is now called multitasking. He loved being both director and performer. His directorial flashes of genius, and they were that, I know have been described and minutely analyzed elsewhere, so I'll not attempt it here. However, I had the chance to observe his acting performances eight times a week. His intense feeling and magisterial voice, which could range from a whisper to a commanding roar, were exciting to audiences. It was on radio, where shows usually had only one performance, that he could mesmerize an entire network with never a letdown, and opening night was also closing night, but in the theater once he had settled into the run he would sometimes coast. During one matinee he became so introspective in one of Brutus' soliloquies that an audience member in the balcony called out, "Louder!" On the radio, where actors learn to essentially play to one person, Orson was always riveting, but it did not always work in theater.

The opening on November 11 was a brilliant success. Orson and the Mercury were cleverly playing on the public's nervousness about international tensions in Europe, and the possibility of war. The male leads in the cast were all costumed in military uniforms resembling those of Fascist Italy. Indeed, some of the publicity sub-heads read *Death of a Dictator. Caesar* is one of Shakespeare's most exciting plays. Many cuts were made. There was no intermission, and the excitement built without letup to the end, when Marc Antony speaks his eulogy for Brutus:

> This was the noblest Roman of them all.
> All the conspirators, save only he,
> Did that they did in envy of Great Caesar;
> He, only in general honest thought,
> And common good to all, made one of them.
> His life was gentle, and the elements so mix'd in
> him, that Nature might stand up,
> And say to all the world, 'This was a man!'

. . . while lights set in the floor of the two platforms came up full, pointing straight up, enveloping George Coulouris and the others in brilliant light. It was a dramatic tableau and a great curtain.

Enthusiastic press notices the next morning included these:

"Liberates Shakespeare From The Strait-Jacket Tradition. Something deathless and dangerous in the world sweeps past you down the darkened aisles of the Mercury." (John Mason Brown — *New York Post*). "The Most Exhilarating Play In New York." (Heywood Broun — *The World-Telegram*).

It was obvious the seats in the little Mercury Theater would be filled for some time to come.

For many decades Western Union telegrams were the traditional way for friends to wish the actors well on opening night. The ones I got that November 11 are still in my scrapbook — from the Let's Pretenders and from family friends. The most touching and heart-warming wire, though, was from my parents. It read:

MAY THE SUN SHINE ON YOUR ROAD AHEAD.
MUMMY AND DADDY

The Tent Scene.

Instead of resting after its success, the Mercury got busier. Less than six weeks later, Thomas Dekker's hearty, bawdy Elizabethan comedy, *The Shoemakers' Holiday*, opened on January 1, 1938, exactly 338 years after its first performance at the English Court in 1600. The complicated plot involves a nobleman who tricks the girl he would like to marry into believing that her fiancé is dead. The shoemakers, though, discover the plot, and declare a pancake holiday. I was billed as "A Boy" and spoke the prologue: "Kind friends and honest boon companions. I present you here with a merrie-conceited comedy . . . ," and recited a summary of the plot which had been, for pace and comedy, vastly cut. The show, again without intermission, lasted just an hour and a quarter.

Shoemaker was, of course, directed by Orson, who also designed the set. A burlap cyclorama now covered the back wall. The ramp from *Caesar*, which had been angled upstage, was now turned around

Shoemakers' Holiday. Norman Lloyd, Arthur Anderson, Hiram (Chubby) Sherman Costume designer Milia Davenport bought Chubby's hat from me for five dollars.

to face the audience, and covered with straw matting. Simple wood-slat suggestions of houses ranged up and down its length, with inner stages left and right. Each inner stage had a curtain which could be opened or closed instantly. The Rome of *Julius Caesar* had been transformed into Elizabethan London, and the playing tempo almost doubled.

New York notices were also very upbeat, with quotes such as: "A merry ribald antic. The funniest jog of the season." (Brooks Atkinson — *New York Times*), and "Full twenty-four hours have passed since the curtain fell and we are still laughing." (Sidney Whipple — *World-Telegram*). We played *Shoemaker's Holiday* in repertory with *Caesar* for 68 performances.

Once *Shoemaker* had opened, yet another Mercury project appeared: *The Worklight Theatre*. This was a series of readings of new scripts on the Mercury stage, literally under a work light, done on Sundays, our dark night. One of them was *Dear Abigail*, by David Howard. The characters included a retired New England sea captain, played by Parker Fennelly, his daughter Abigail, Edith Barrett, and her fifteen-year-old nephew Joel, the part obviously written for me. Abigail was sweetness and light on the outside, but the audience knew her to be scheming and evil. I thought it was a good drama, but unfortunately, it was never heard of again. Lillian Hellman, of course, made a great success with the same kind of character a year later, in 1939.

Because there was no scenery, lights had to be doused in the dressing rooms during every performance at the Mercury, and as we settled into the run of *Caesar* everyone got used to working in the dark. We all learned to feel our way up and down the metal stairs. As I was a student at PCS I tried to do my homework during stage waits with the aid of an electric lantern which had a tiny bulb at the bottom, but soon found it impossible, probably one reason it took me five years to get through high school.

Lucius' early scenes were to bring the conspirators in to Brutus' orchard where they planned the assassination, and so my dialogue was minimal. Another conspirator, Ligarius, arrives later, and my line to Brutus was, "Here is a sick man who would speak with you."

This went well enough except for one matinee when I simply forgot my entrance. That evening at half hour I overheard Stefan

Schnabel, in the dressing room across the hall from mine, say, "Perhaps we'll hear 'Here is a sick man who would speak with you' tonight." I got up from my chair. Chubby Sherman, with whom I shared the dressing room, said quietly, "Don't say anything, Arthur." But I charged across the hall and said self-righteously, "For whose ears was that intended?" There was a long, tense silence, then Stefan said, "Our smart young friend here." It was one of my few unpleasant moments at the Mercury, and of course I had created it myself.

The only really unfortunate thing that happened during the play's run did not involve me. It was one night during the assassination scene. "Hence! Wilt thou lift up Olympus?" says Caesar, as the conspirators close in with their knives. "Speak, hands for me!" says Brutus. Caesar: "Et tu, Brute? Then fall, Caesar." Stage direction: *Dies.* And Caesar falls, mortally wounded. There was an instant blackout as pandemonium reigned in Rome. The Hammond organ played all its bass notes, and the citizens were heard roaring in the darkness. It is civil war. It was great theater, enough to send shivers up anyone's spine.

To avoid accidents all the conspirators had rubber knives. Orson's, however, was real — a gleaming steel stag-handled knife, and this time when he stabbed Caesar, Joseph Holland, who played the role, was wounded in an artery, on the inside of his upper arm. One of the actors said that in the darkness he thought that someone was peeing on him, but it was Joe Holland's blood. He was hustled out the stage door and to a hospital. When I saw Orson Welles in his dressing room later, he had a large bottle of Scotch in front of him. He thought he had killed Joe Holland. The wound was not fatal, but I would venture to guess that the scene was later re-staged, or at least with a different knife.

I got along well with the other Mercury actors, especially Alice Frost, now playing the part of Portia, Brutus' wife, with whom I'd worked in radio. She would wait stage left for her first entrance, in a beautiful long green night robe. But Alice was hard of hearing, and so every performance I would tap her shoulder when it was time to enter.

The only person with whom I didn't get along well, for some reason, was Martin Gabel, who played Cassius. Our personalities just seemed to grate on each other. One night I brought a lemon and sucked it in the wings to make his mouth pucker up. This didn't affect him, however, as he had a different handicap. He was nearsighted, and so the lemon was wasted.

It should be said, though, that Mr. Gabel was brilliant in the play. He was stocky and fairly short, not right for what Caesar describes as "the lean and hungry Cassius."

But it did not matter. He had the bite and the energy and the drive it needed, for Cassius is the one who drives the plot, and convinces Brutus to join the conspiracy.

The next Mercury event was its own production of *The Cradle Will Rock* (not the one that had been aborted by the Government.) It had been tried out for four Sundays as a production of the *Worklight Theatre*. It opened at the Windsor Theater on January 3, two days after *Shoemakers' Holiday*, and ran for 108 performances. On April 29 Orson opened George Bernard Shaw's *Heartbreak House*, starring himself as Captain Shotover, at the Mercury, while Caesar had moved a block west to the National (now the Nederlander). There were suitable publicity shots of our actors putting up a new sign on West 41st Street that read *MERCURY STREET*.

The National was more modern and less friendly than the Mercury, but had 500 more seats, and thus potentially much better grosses than our original home. My dressing room was three flights up, and I was all alone in there.

Frankly, it was boring. My scenes in the play were brief, and separated by a long interval during which there was literally nothing to do. During the Wednesday matinee of March 10, my eye lit upon the sprinkler heads on the ceiling, and I asked myself what would happen when heat was applied to the alloy, which was supposed to ooze down, I understood, in case of a fire. I stood on a chair and applied a match to the sprinkler head, expecting to see the ooze.

Instead, the sprinkler head popped off as it was designed to do, and a powerful spray of water spewed out. There was no turning it off. The only thing to do was to notify the stagehands below to see if they could take care of it.

My hair and my costume were soaked. I raced down the stairs to the basement where the stagehands were playing their usual game of poker. My voice went into falsetto and I gasped, "The sprinkler! The sprinkler!" I was finally able to make them understand what had happened. At this the oldest stagehand *slowly* rose from his chair, *slowly* went to a tool closet, *slowly* unlocked it and got a wrench, and *slowly* went to a valve and turned off the water.

Meanwhile, all hell had broken out upstairs. The water from the dressing room was pouring out from under a metal fire door directly down onto the main switchboard, so the electricians, no doubt to save their own lives, pulled all the dimmer switches. This put the stage in semi-darkness, and the water started to pool downstage where Orson was beginning his funeral oration. He climbed down from the pulpit and the stagehands mopped the floor, and the Hammond organ played some music, whether Shakespearean or not I do not know.

It was at least fifteen minutes before the play resumed, and finally Walter Ash, the stage manager, instructed the actors to get back onstage. As I stood in the hallway on stage level, in a state of shock as I recall, Martin Gabel came downstairs and said to me with a satisfied smile, "WELL, Mr. Anderson!"

Somehow, I got to do the tent scene with Orson, and the song, on automatic pilot I suppose. Finally the matinee was over. As I recall I phoned my mother to tell her what had happened, and she came to take me home. But before I could go I was summoned to the theater office by Orson Welles and John Houseman, who sat at a desk with grave faces. They said this was a serious situation and that they could have had me fired or suspended me, but my understudy, Edgie Paul, was not up in the part, and I'd have to go on that night.

This could not go unpunished, though. My penalty was that for the next two weeks I could not go anywhere in the theater except onstage without being followed by one of the extras. This was ignominious enough, but I also had to pay him a dollar a performance. My punishment was public or at least semi-public disgrace, and a quite suitable one it was.

Whether Orson and Mr. Houseman fell over laughing when I left the office I do not know, but it did have its serious aspect. By the grace of God there was a device which automatically notified the fire department if a sprinkler went off, and this was not working. A positive side, though, was that the incident made every one of the New York dailies. The headline in *The New York Sun* was:

Bill for damages--National Theatre

to Arthur Anderson
Pay to Paddy Carroll

For:

Porters, cleaners, etc.
replacement of sprinkler head

Prop Department Damage
Electrical Department Damage

$30.00

Paid in full

George Zorn

Receipted bill for the sprinkler damage.

THOSE ROMANS COULD TAKE IT
ASK LUCIUS — HE KNOWS

During my time with the Mercury, and later, researching this book, I learned something of the lives of some of my fellow actors, and their later careers, which took them in many directions. The one who later went on to the greatest success was, of course, Joseph Cotten. Before the Mercury he had done two Broadway plays, the WPA productions of *Horse Eats Hat*, then *Doctor Faustus*, both directed by Orson Welles. Faustus presented a problem for Orson, however, because of the WPA, created by Franklin Roosevelt during the Depression. It was supposed to give jobs and income to the unemployed, of whom there were thousands. Joe, however, was doing very well in radio, but Orson wanted him for the show, and so the program for *Doctor Faustus* read: *Second Scholar: Joseph Wooll.*

Joe and I liked each other. Besides being one of the conspirators in *Caesar*, he played the romantic lead opposite Ruth Ford in *Shoemaker*. Once I had spoken the prologue, I had very few lines as Boy. This was frustrating. In the last scene I was supposed to come down the ramp and, without a word, present ceremonial robes to Whitford Kane, who as Simon Eyre had just been appointed Lord Mayor of London. At the last performance I indulged myself, coming down the ramp and singing out: "Here be the raiments, Sir!" Joe Cotten, facing upstage, said sotto voce in his Virginia accent, with mock disgust, "Heah be the raiments . . ."

Besides Joseph Cotten, who started his trip to stardom in *The Philadelphia Story* with Katharine Hepburn, Orson later cast several other Mercury actors in *Citizen Kane*, including George Coulouris, Ray Collins, William Alland and Agnes Moorehead, who later had her own brilliant stage success in Shaw's *Don Juan in Hell*. Ray appeared on stage in *Native Son*, directed by Orson in 1941, and in television was a long-time featured player on *Perry Mason*. William Alland, besides playing small parts in *Caesar* and *Shoemakers' Holiday*, was also a valuable all-round assistant to Orson on *The Mercury Theatre on the Air* on radio, where Orson referred to him as Vachtangov. During afternoon rehearsals, Studio 1 would echo with *Vachtangov! Bring me my pineapple juice!* He later became a Hollywood producer of several important films.

Originally a Mercury extra, William Herz worked in the Mercury office. He later became co-owner of The Stony Creek Theater, and then went on to a long-term relationship with The Actors' Fund.

Sneden's Landing
N.Y.

Christmas 1937

We hope you are well. Virginia's self-portrait (above)
may give you some notion of how we are doing in case you
didn't know. In the meantime, Merry Christmas to you
from Budget, Orson, Virginia and .... Christopher

Orson's Christmas card.

Richard Barr also worked in the office, and brought Orson his lunches from Longchamps'. Dick Barr later became a Broadway and off-Broadway producer, and years later employed me more than once.

Francis Carpenter, who played Dodger in *Shoemakers' Holiday*, later distinguished himself in an entirely different way. In World War II he was a Seaman First Class, and was chosen to land in the US invasion of Sicily, as he knew the island from having vacationed there. He came upon eight terrified peasants in a cornfield, and as *Variety* described it: ". . . located two important roads, captured two Italian soldiers, discovered a large minefield and wound up drinking wine with the peasants, who gave him valuable information, and he later sang for them an aria from *Rigoletto*. For his accomplishments Francis Carpenter was recommended for The Navy Cross."

My most enduring friendship from The Mercury, which lasts to this day, is with Kevin O'Morrison, who then billed himself as Kent Adams. Kevin, a fresh-faced young juvenile, had arrived from St. Louis in 1937 with fifty dollars, enough for a week's rent at the YMCA, and great hopes of making a success on Broadway. He saw Orson at the Maxine Elliott Theater, where he was playing the lead in *Doctor Faustus*, went backstage and asked for work. Orson told him he was thinking of founding his own theater, and to come back when that happened. Kevin did join The Mercury in 1937, acted in *Caesar, Shoemakers' Holiday*, and worked in the office. Though he and Bill Herz collected pictures and resumes from hopeful actors, it was, of course, Orson who made all the casting decisions. Kevin O'Morrison later became an important playwright, about which more later. Martin Gabel did very well both before and after The Mercury. In 1936 he had originated the role of Dr. John Wayne, the male lead in the radio daytime serial *Big Sister*, and played it for years. He acted in seventeen plays on Broadway and then became the producer of nine more. He was also an astute investor, and had a large stake in Howard Lindsay's hit production *Life With Father*.

Norman Lloyd, who played Cinna the Poet in *Caesar* and Firk in *Shoemakers' Holiday*, was brought to Hollywood by Orson to appear in *Heart of Darkness*, which was shelved by RKO. He later achieved great acting success in Hollywood films, playing a big role in the Alfred Hitchcock film *Saboteur*, and played Dr. Auschlander in the hospital drama *St. Elsewhere* on television. Years later he was Associate Producer for an entire season of *Alfred Hitchcock Presents*.

Elliott Reid was called Ted by his fellow actors. He was only seventeen when he played Cinna the Conspirator. He was over six feet tall, and in entertainments in the tiny Professional Children's School auditorium had had to stand in front of the stage — not on it. Otherwise, his head would have disappeared in the teaser curtain. After The Mercury he did six more Broadway productions, three of them being musicals or revues, as Ted had an innate talent for comedy, and did faultless impersonations of famous people. He played The Radio City Music Hall for six weeks doing all the radio news commentators of the day, and later was called by President Kennedy to impersonate him at a Washington Gridiron Club dinner. In 1960 Ted moved to the West Coast, and he had a successful film career. Cinna the Conspirator had been only the beginning.

John Berry, one of the extras in *Caesar*, became an important Hollywood film director, and Joseph Holland, who played the title role in *Caesar*, appeared in 21 other Broadway plays between 1934 and 1957.

Hiram Sherman, whom we all knew as Chubby, besides The Mercury did more than 25 plays and six musicals on Broadway, the last ones having been *How Now Dow Jones* and *Anne of Green Gables* in 1969. From what I have been able to determine he eventually went to live with an aunt in Ohio, his birthplace.

Chubby Sherman was an actors' actor, loved by many theater people for his persona, which was a mixture of innocent country bumpkin and sharp wit. Chubby was for some years on the Council of Actors' Equity. He was confronted once by a fellow Council member, who asked him, *Are you a Communist?* His reply was, *We're not supposed to say*, thus leaving his questioner completely in the dark. A more direct answer was when Chubby helped write a resolution in 1941 barring "members of the Communist, Nazi or Fascist parties or their sympathizers from holding office in or being employed by Actors' Equity."

Chubby and I had the Mercury in common, and remained friends for many years. It was ten years after *Caesar* that he was back at the National in a short-lived play called *Town House*, which opened there in September 1948. He sent me a postcard which read,

"Many thanks for your wire. The National Theatre isn't the place it was ten years ago . . . . I miss all that water cascading down."

Caesar closed at The National May 25, 1938. After Orson had left the cast to become Captain Shotover in Shaw's *Heartbreak House,* it featured Tom Powers as Brutus. I remember his Brutus as a good, earnest performance, but he did not have half the pent-up energy or the vocal dynamics in the role as did Orson Welles.

I went back to my pre-Mercury routine: school in the daytime, plus more *Let's Pretend, American School of the Air* and other radio shows. On weekends I would often go out to Staten Island and ride my bike, which I was able to keep at our old house. I did not know if I'd see any of the Mercury people ever again. As things turned out I did see some of them quite soon.

5
CHAPTER
MORE OF THE MERCURY

The summer of 1938, by pure happenstance, worked out better than I could have hoped for. I had signed up again to go to Camp Anchorage on Trout Lake, but this time things did not go well there. I got in trouble with one of the counselors. I had started to climb a tree, and he told me not to. A few minutes later I did anyway, and was sent home.

Meanwhile, that summer was a busy one for the Mercury Theatre. One of Orson's projects was a revival of the William Gillette farce *Too Much Johnson* at the Stony Creek Conn. Theater. Stony Creek is on the Connecticut shore, 85 miles from New York. It faces Long Island Sound and has a good view of the water, and of the tiny Thimble Islands. They are desirable pieces of real estate, even though most of them seem to consist mostly of a huge boulder sticking up out of the ocean, and are big enough for only one house. The town of Stony Creek has boat moorings, restaurants, tennis courts and fishing docks, but at low tide the waterfront has little more than fragrant seaweed and mud flats.

The theater, built as a silent movie house in the early 1900s, was originally called The Lyric. A community theater group purchased it in the 1920s and named it The Stony Creek Theater. In collaboration with Lee Shubert they did the original production of *Death Takes a Holiday*, later a big success on Broadway. The wooden building, with peaked roof, could not have held an audience of more than 200.

Stony Creek was a good place to escape from the city's heat, a respite from my disappointing camp experience and a place to be with many of my friends from the Mercury. I don't believe I had been cast in a play there, but after I arrived I was given a part in the Stony Creek Theater's production of *Gold in the Hills or the Dead Sister's Secret*, a takeoff on the melodramas of the 1890s, complete with olios between the acts. An olio, used in earlier theater, was a musical act played downstage "in one" before a canvas backdrop, while the scenery was being set for the next act of the play. The summer theater was being run by Alan Fishburn and Orson's Mercury assistant, William (Bill) Herz, who hadn't done much acting but was in love with theater. I was cast as Little Tommy, for which I was wildly unsuitable, but, the play being a satire, that did not matter.

Kevin O'Morrison of the Mercury was also there, and I felt I knew him well enough to play a joke on him. He was cast as a derelict, passed out from liquor, with his head on a table in front of a window which, this being summer stock, had no panes. I found a cigarette and blew smoke in his face. Being a trouper Kevin did not move, but well knowing who must have done it took me over his knee and spanked me when the scene was over.

In July was the opening of *Too Much Johnson*, which was done in three acts, and had a two-week run. To expedite the scene changes it was Orson's idea to substitute, instead of curtains opening and closing, a group of Negro slaves, of which I volunteered to be one, crossing the stage in lock-step and singing:

> "Way (step) down upon the Swannee River (step)
> Far (step), far away (step, step, step) . . ."

Orson Welles was simultaneously doing his weekly *Mercury Theater on the Air* on CBS Radio. On many, even most occasions he had Paul Stewart, Richard Wilson and others read his lines and direct rehearsals, and often did the broadcast reading the script "cold," almost without rehearsal. But it was, of course, obligatory for him to get to the studio for the broadcast. I do not know who fomented the story of Orson's chartering a trolley car to take him from Branford to the New Haven station to make his train to New York, but like so many Orson Welles stories it is apocryphal. Actually, Bill Herz tells me, during the Stony Creek weeks he always had a car at his disposal.

Most of the Playhouse actors lived at the Flying Point Hotel, on a grassy knoll overlooking the Sound. Almost directly in front of it was an old barge, beached on the shore, on which sat a tall derrick, used many years before to lift huge blocks of stone which came from the quarry that gave the town its name. It was a rotting eyesore, but nobody seemed to mind. The Flying Point was an aging white clapboard structure. The front porch ran the entire width of the building, with many rocking chairs. It was what an old-fashioned resort should look like. It was lovely but, Bill Herz said, infested with insects. I didn't see any of those, but I do remember that when I awoke in the morning the insides of my shoes would be green with mold.

In mid-July I was back in New York. The Mercury contract with the Columbia Broadcasting System had originally been for a series of radio plays called *First Person Singular*, but no doubt due to the Mercury's and Orson's growing publicity it became *The Mercury Theater on the Air*. The title was changed, but not the format. Orson Welles was always the narrator, and as such played the leading role.

Treasure Island was supposed to be the first broadcast on July 11, but it was put off and Bram Stoker's *Dracula* became the opening show. They finally got to *Treasure Island* on the 18th, and it was one of my most thrilling radio experiences, before or after. The Robert Louis Stevenson story is exciting, and so was the radio adaptation. I played young Jim Hawkins, and did some of the narration, while Orson took over the later narration and also played the villainous Long John Silver. And we had Agnes Moorehead as my mother, Alfred Shirley as Doctor Livesy, Eustace Wyatt as the Squire and Ray Collins as crazy old Ben Gunn. The CBS sound people, Ray Kremer and Ora Nichols, the only female sound effects artist in that Golden Age of Radio, were at their best, and Brad Barker played the parrot ("Awk! Pieces of eight! Pieces of eight! Awk!"). Bernard Herrman adapted the music and conducted a full orchestra. The Mercury theme music was *Tchaikovsky's Piano Concerto in B Flat Minor*.

The end of the program brought me some extra publicity, not necessarily welcome, due to my exploit with the sprinkler that past March. Orson had some time to fill for his closing, and ad libbed the following: "I'd like you to meet Jim Hawkins Junior. Our leading man is 15 years old. Last season he made a really startling contribution to the stage history of Shakespeare's plays. This was during the course of some experiments with the Mercury Theater sprinkler system. In consequence of what must have been extensive research in that field he caused it to rain — actually to rain — and copiously to rain where in more than 300 years it had never rained in *Julius Caesar* before. It rained on Brutus. It rained all over Brutus in the forum. I was Brutus and I ought to know. As dramatic criticism I found it telling, and even final. Our popular leading man says he did it all with a match. I don't dare to think what he'll do when he's old enough to run for President. But meanwhile no matter what happens to the plumbing he can always work at the Mercury."

The most famous, or infamous, Mercury broadcast was, of course, the October 30 adaptation of H.G. Wells' *War of the Worlds*, brought up to date and transported from England to Grover's Mills, New Jersey, which terrified many people who had not heard the beginning, having just switched over from an NBC broadcast because they did not care to hear the singer Nelson Eddy. I wasn't called for that as there were no teenaged parts in it. I was riding my bicycle on Staten Island that day. Because of the ensuing publicity, the Mercury program gained a sponsor and on December 9 became *The Campbell (Soup) Playhouse*. Ernest Chappell was the rich-voiced announcer (they were never called "Spokesmen" in those days).

Other Mercury roles I was called for that season included young Clarence in *Life With Father*, Billy The Post Boy in *Sherlock Holmes* and The Ghost Of Christmas Past in *A Christmas Carol*, done on December 20th. Frankly, I was surprised to be cast in that part, but Dickens does describe The Ghost of Christmas Past as a *young* ghost.

All these shows were done in Studio 1, at that time the network's largest. I was and still am awed by the fact that each time in that same room I found myself in a completely different world, on such programs as *Let's Pretend* (dramatized children's fairy tales on Saturday mornings,) *Aunt Jenny's Real Life Stories* (Monday through Friday) "Presented by Spry, The All-Vegetable Shortening," and *The Mercury Theatre on the Air*, a night-time drama series. Each had its own loyal audience. Such was the great color and diversity of radio programming at the time. Different worlds are created, too, with each new performance on a theater stage or in a film studio. Perhaps that is what makes them all so fascinating.

In August 1938 I turned sixteen. Those early days of my career were, as I look back on them, charmed. I was part of a network of friends and mentors, and radio directors who called me regularly. This was not always to be, of course. Also, I had no major expenses. I did not even pay my parents board until I came home from military service.

Other Mercury productions that autumn included *Danton's Death* with Vladimir Sokoloff, a celebrated Russian actor who as one of the leading members of the proletariat had as one critic called it, bitter criticism of "pipple in walwit robes."

I think I was lucky there were no parts for me in *Five Kings*, the Mercury's slowly unfolding 1939 disaster which took place in both Philadelphia and Boston. If I had been offered one I am sure I would have taken it and this, with weeks' long engagements in those cities, would have disrupted my school work without helping me develop as an actor.

After the broadcast of *A Christmas Carol* my only contact with The Mercury Theatre was when they were ensconced in Hollywood, where Orson was now filming *Citizen Kane* and *The Magnificent Ambersons*, and sandwiching in Mercury radio broadcasts as well. I remember writing to Orson, asking him if there might be anything for me in one of his films. Richard Wilson sent me a letter in reply, a courtesy unusual in the film capital. He was sorry that there was nothing, he wrote, but they'd, of course, keep me in mind. I did not know whether to be amused or distressed by my older brother George who said, "Why don't you go out to Hollywood and work with Orson Welles in pictures?" Young as I was I had enough show-business savvy to know that just isn't the way it's done.

The Mercury Theatre was a marvelous part of my young actor's life. I have always been proud of that credit, and whenever I send my picture to a casting director it is still included in my resume.

6
CHAPTER
STAGE AND RADIO IN MY TEENS

My adolescence, like those of most children, was not always comfortable or joyful. Shortly after joining *Let's Pretend* I went into my awkward years, not knowing whether I was a child or a grownup, and not feeling I fitted into either category. My voice started changing as well — serious for a child radio actor. When I was called for an afternoon or an evening program, I knew I could carry off the 12-year-old and younger parts I was cast in, but a morning show was a problem. I knew nothing about voice warm-ups, of course. That was another reason I felt secure and happy on *Let's Pretend*. When doing a giant or an enchanted frog, adolescent voice change did not matter. I was gangling and bony, with a sensitive face, wavy brown hair and slightly protruding ears.

In those days I masked my insecurity and shyness by clowning — doing vocal sound effects and acting silly at parties, where I felt particularly vulnerable. For better or worse I also had a lively sense of mischief, or at least experimentation. This, of course, had gotten me in big trouble during *Caesar*, but none of my shenanigans were ever spiteful or mean-spirited. I remember a drinking cup dispenser in the basement of the Little Theatre (now the Helen Hayes), where CBS was broadcasting *The American School of the Air*, presided over that day by Dorothy Gordon. When you pressed a button, a small Dixie cup would drop onto a hook . . . POK! I was trying out this wonderful sound while Miss Gordon was rehearsing . . . . POK! . . . POK! Finally, she said, "Nila, I simply cannot . . ." and after two words from Nila Mack it was over.

Then there was the recording session at the RCA studios on East 24th Street. These were 15-minute dramatizations for Lifebuoy Soap.

In those days, long before tape was invented, there was tension, because if an actor made a mistake at any point the wax disk had to be scrapped and the whole record started over again. Paul Stewart was in most of these. It was an exhausting all-day session. He stretched out on three folding chairs for a nap. Mickey O'Day and I woke him, pointing frantically to the script. He leaped up to the microphone, but, of course, he was not in that episode at all. It was, I admit, rotten.

In 1938 CBS, short of studio space, was now broadcasting *Let's Pretend* on late weekday afternoons from the venerable Liederkranz Hall on East 58th Street. An upstairs ballroom was now a radio studio, and the crystal chandeliers had been replaced with basketball lights with wire guards. The place was esthetically ruined, but the acoustics were fine for radio. Meanwhile, the Liederkranz Club still maintained its German-flavored dining room below. Once, during a rehearsal break, Michael O'Day and I peered over the oak banister and saw an old, bald German waiter two floors below stacking his plates, ready to fill them with wiener schnitzel from the fragrant kitchen. We dropped little drops of water from Dixie cups, then dropped more as the old waiter, perplexed, wiped the wet plates. When the break was over, an announcement came from the control room that whoever was doing this had better cut it out.

Another satisfying occupation was when publicity photos were being taken in the studios at 485 Madison Avenue. I would drop used photographers' flash bulbs down an unoccupied air shaft, and each made a satisfying pop as it exploded 22 floors below. Though the mischief was minor and mostly harmless, I suppose it was part of my growing up in radio — perhaps a substitute for companionship I didn't have. I did not play ball with the kids on the block — I didn't even know the kids on the block. My life centered around school, and acting.

The Andersons did not take vacation trips, except for some wonderful times at the house of my Uncle Charles on the Connecticut seashore near Niantic. One summer, while I was there without my parents, I had to let them know I'd be in New York the following week as I had been called for the daytime serial *Big Sister*, sponsored by Rinso. I prepared to send a telegram, but didn't know whether to word it "IN BIG SISTER," "ON BIG SISTER" or "DOING

BIG SISTER." Any of them, I thought, would sound incestuous to the Western Union operator. How I solved that I do not remember.

Being at that time mostly a radio actor, I learned various techniques by osmosis — just by doing radio. Most of the microphones, for instance, were RCA Type 44 models called ribbon mikes. A delicate metal ribbon would vibrate when a sound was fed into the mike. That generated a minute electrical current, which was then amplified. Actors liked those mikes because two people could work on each side without crowding. You learned how to fade in or fade out by moving nearer or farther from the mike, and this became second nature to experienced radio performers.

Once Bob Steel, then director of *Aunt Jenny's Real Life Stories*, had the idea of using an overhead mike, so that the actors could relate to each other in a scene without having a piece of equipment in front of them. This did not work, however. When actors really saw and related to each other, as on stage or in films, they would lose their places in the script — not good on radio.

Like most radio actors I was called by various directors in my teenage years. Among them, besides Nila Mack, was another CBS director, Earle McGill. He was enormously experienced and knowledgeable, and had a sense of humor as well. One *School of the Air* show he directed was a group of high-school girls discussing some important issue. While they sat at the microphones waiting for the roundtable program to begin, they started discussing the attractiveness of various studio personnel. "I could really go for that announcer," said one. "He's handsome." Another said, "Wouldn't it be terrible if they could hear us in there?" Earle pressed the talkback and said, "No, go right ahead. We can't hear a word you're saying." I wondered at being told that Earle McGill spoke Yiddish fluently, but later found it was because he had grown up in the Lower East Side tenement district.

I was one of the many New York radio actors who loved working for Charles Warburton, who was British through and through. He had played and directed at The Old Vic in Stratford-Upon-Avon, and done four Broadway plays. He then evidently decided that radio acting, and then directing was a more dependable way of earning a living. Others I have talked to all remember his directing a soupy, mawkish daytime drama whose name is lost to antiquity.

Never did he utter a word to criticize the material. He took a fatherly interest in young actresses, gently chiding them with "Don't be a little noodle, my dear."

As the cast sat at the table for the first reading he would time the music bridges, stopwatch in hand, by intoning, "Tiddly bum, tiddly bum, tiddly bum, CUE." Charlie Warburton would always preface the air show by saying, "Let's pop it." If the show had pleased him he would say, "We rejoice in good health and in the sight of God and man."

Doing a daytime serial was not complicated, as were some of the evening shows, which had full orchestras and sometimes complicated sound effects. Everyone knew what to do, and it all worked very smoothly. So smoothly, in fact, that once during an *Aunt Jenny* broadcast I looked up and saw John Loveton, the director, practicing golf swings in the control room.

Network directors usually had final say on the casting of their shows, unlike those put on by ad agencies. Once David Howard, who was on staff at NBC, had done weeks of research on an important drama — something like *The History of the United States* or some such. Before first rehearsal he asked the director, Harry MacFayden, who he had cast in the leading roles. Harry said, "Well, I've just gotten some of the boys and girls together, to see who can play what." David was furious, but there was nothing he could do.

All of radio being live in that Golden Age there were, of course, inevitable temporary brain glitches which caused actors to commit what are often called bloopers, or fluffs. The results could be hilarious, obscene, or just confusing. I will not bore the reader by repeating the old classics such as "Hoobert Heever" and "Artrusco Turanini," but here are a few additions to that folklore.

The first was made by Julian Noa, who had a reputation for playing cantankerous old men. On one broadcast he said a wrong word, corrected it, and when the correction sounded worse, reinstated the original bobble. It was this:

> "Oh, poppycack."
> . . . Err, cock.
> NO, CACK!"

You wouldn't think that an announcer couldn't even say the name of the station right, but it happened one day in Chicago. NBC in those days had two networks, the Red and the Blue, and announcers might do station breaks on one or the other, as assigned. This particular announcer stepped up to the microphone at the little wall desk, pushed the button to ring the familiar NBC chimes, and the following came out:

"WMAQ, Chicago."
(A pause.)
"No-o-o, this is WENR, Chicago."
(A longer pause.)
"No, by God, this *IS* WMAQ, Chicago!"

He was fired the next day.

Then there was the announcer who proudly billboarded a weekly program sponsored by Bond Bread thus:

"Ladies and gentlemen — the Blonde Bed Breakers are on the air!"

Two that I heard myself were on New York stations, the first by an announcer on our august classical music station WQXR:

"And now, the Mozart Piano Concerto In Flea Bat Minor."

And quite recently, while working on this book, I heard a meteorologist on WCBS confidently predict:

". . . and this afternoon we'll have shattered scowers."

In the autumn of 1938 I had the security of radio work and the involvement at school to keep me busy. Added to that was another production of *Julius Caesar* on NBC's experimental television station, WNBT, again in Studio 3-H. I was still Brutus' page boy Lucius, but without the song, of course. The lights were super-hot and the camera work primitive. My record book shows that there were two

The Let's Pretenders. Back row: Arthur Anderson, Gwen Davies, Jack Grimes, Bill Lipton, Miriam Wolfe. Front row: Michael O'Day, Betty Janer Tyler, Nila Mack, Sybil Trent.

camera days and the play, live of course, was telecast on November 20. This time my fee was $25, less than for *The Still Alarm*

In those early days of television very few people had sets. If a New York actor's family or friends wanted to see his performance, they would pay admission at the Guild Newsreel Theater on West 50th Street, opposite the RCA Building. The set was in the basement lounge. The screen was small, the pictures fuzzy, and one actor cracked that it made everybody look like Jed Harris, a Broadway producer who was far from good-looking and not universally well liked.

Whatever else was happening, or not happening in my career, for eighteen years there was always *Let's Pretend*. I had auditioned for Nila Mack in May, 1936 and, except for my time in the armed forces was on almost every broadcast until the last, on October 23, 1954. *Let's Pretend* and its forerunner, *The Adventures of Helen and Mary*, lasted for almost 25 years on the CBS Network. They were loved by children and their parents, and were a proud chapter in radio's history.

Let's Pretend has also been the source of some of my closest friendships, and they have all lasted for many years. One of the first was with Sybil Trent. At age six she had her own radio program, *Sybil Elaine and Her Kiddie Revue*, and was then in Billy Rose's extravaganza *Jumbo*, starring Jimmy Durante, at the huge Hippodrome Theater. The Rodgers and Hart classic *Little Girl Blue* was sung to Sybil, who entered in a silver and crystal coach drawn by two white ponies, and exited riding on an elephant. When I came aboard, she had already been on *Pretend* for a year, and her many other radio roles included emotional leads on daytime serials. For Nila Mack she played everything from beautiful princesses in danger to tiny elves. We were both part of the *Let's Pretend* family, and saw and worked together every week for 18 years (the program did not take a summer hiatus as did most radio shows.) Sybil had a warm personality and a lovely singing voice, and it was she who sang the lead in the duet *Cream Of Wheat Is So Good To Eat, Yes, We Have It Ev'ry Day . . . ."* In 1948 she, Don Hughes and I packaged a light comedy program with songs for TV called *Date For Three*. We thought it was delightful, but no takers.

Our friendship continued as Sybil married Andrew Nieporent, and she was so proud of her two sons, Drew, who is a prominent restaurateur and President of Myriad Restaurant Group, and his brother Tracy, who is Vice President and Director of Marketing. In 1960 Sybil shifted from acting to casting. She was a successful agent, then a casting director at Young & Rubicam for 23 years. During Sybil's last illness in 2000 I stuffed her folding wheelchair into the trunk of our little Dodge Aries to take her to and from her hospital treatments.

Donald Hughes was five years older than I. He had a distinctive radio voice with an edge to it, and on *Let's Pretend* Nila cast him in parts ranging from wise councilors to dastardly villains. His mother had been a ballet dancer in vaudeville, and Don moved with a dancer's grace. He began acting in plays at age eight, then in radio. He and I shared a similar sense of humor, and when during rehearsal I would draw a cartoon based on the story he would dash off a verse to go with it. We were friends from my first days on the program, and this continued during my hitch in the US Air Force, and his in the Infantry in Europe.

After I married Alice, he and his wife Ann, another PCS'er, would celebrate his Hallowe'en birthday with us, and then we'd sing carols together the Saturday before Christmas — yearly rituals which we all enjoyed. Don's talent as a writer developed early, and when radio acting jobs were not enough to support a wife and child he wrote scripts for *Mark Trail*, who was a forest ranger fighting the spoilers and criminals who came into the wilderness. It was produced by another Pretender, Albert Aley.

Radio was a wonderful source of income for Don, as it was for so many of us. He had a brilliantly creative mind, an unusual acting talent and a warm heart. He died in 1990 and Ann within a year later, two great losses to Alice and me.

Miriam Wolfe had also been an original Let's Pretender since 1933. Though a child actor, she said, "I never had a child's voice." She had already amazed Alonzo Dean Cole, producer of *The Witch's Tale*, when he was auditioning replacements for the role of Old Nancy, the title character. Here was a twelve-year-old child with straw hat and bobbed hair, carrying her book bag from school, who stepped up to the microphone with a quavering, toothless delivery, and a cackling, spine-tingling laugh. On our program she also played fairy godmothers, and other mature roles.

Ironically, Miriam and I were friends, but not close ones until after the program had gone off the air, and I found out what a lovely person she was. US dramatic radio having dried up in the mid-1950s, she moved to Canada, where hour-long programs with sound effects and full orchestra were still being done, and in Toronto met and married John Ross, heir to a Canadian brewery fortune. Their marriage was happy, and they produced a son. They visited New York more than once, and Alice and I had a lovely time visiting in Toronto. Her husband pre-deceased Miriam, and she died in 2000.

Besides myself, the only original Let's Pretender surviving is Gwen Davies. While a small child she was given nickels by her mother to put in pay phones at the drugstore and call radio directors to ask for work. She was precocious and peppy, and a talented singer as well as an actor. Gwen started on the program in 1929, at age seven, and developed a radio career in many other shows, including daytime serials such as *Hilltop House*, and nighttime shows including *The Aldrich Family* and *The Kate Smith Hour*. On our show she might be a twinkly elf or a doddering old crone. Besides *Let's Pretend*, Gwen and I were together in *Second Hurricane*, Aaron Copland's play-opera in 1937.

Later, Gwen had two simultaneous careers — as actress and as singer in radio commercials. She and her late husband Larry raised three children. Alice, Amy and I are always welcome at her large stone farmhouse in Bucks County.

A much fuller account of *Let's Pretend*, the people I worked with and loved, and much more about radio in the '30s and '40s are in my book *Let's Pretend and the Golden Age of Radio*, also published by BearManor Media.

AFRA — The American Federation of Radio Artists — was founded in 1937, and negotiated union shop contracts with the networks and ad agencies. That meant you had to be a member of the union to work. That was agreeable to everyone except perhaps some of the employers. There was no suspense or haggling. You knew what you would get. Program fees, which had ranged from disgraceful to so-so, were now uniform, depending on the length of the show and whether it was sustaining (put on by the network) or sponsored, and rehearsal pay depending on the number of hours you rehearsed. A fifteen-minute sponsored program now paid actors $15 plus $6 for the one required hour of rehearsal. At today's prices that, of course, sounds like nothing, but in the mid- and later '30s it was good pay for the time involved. Furthermore, a radio actor if in demand could do four or five shows a day, rehearsal periods being much shorter than on television.

The only exception to these fees was a waiver for programs in which more than 75% of the cast were children, written no doubt to cover kiddie talent shows. But in 1942 most of us on *Let's Pretend* were now in our upper teens, still getting $5, and actual children were only a small part of the cast. I phoned George Heller, AFRA Executive Secretary, and told him of this situation. "Jesus!" he said. "They can't do that to you. I'll see about this, Arthur." On the broadcast of July 11, our fee went up to $10. I am sure CBS told George Heller that if regular sustaining fees had to be paid they'd pull *Let's Pretend* off the air, as there was no income from a sponsor, so this was a compromise — in the network's favor. And that is probably why, in September 1943, *Let's Pretend* began its nine-year sponsorship by Cream of Wheat, with more rehearsal time, original music written by our cellist Maurice Brown, "Uncle" Bill Adams as our host, and broadcasting with a large audience from Playhouse 3, now The Ed Sullivan Theater, where the David Letterman show originates. The AFRA scale for a half-hour commercial show was $47.30 . . . . Without cataloguing all of my radio work between 1935 and 1942, only now do I realize when I look back on it that it was deeply satisfying.

David Howard, being a playwright, knew several literary agents. One of them, a middle-aged man, had offices in the Sardi Building on West 44th Street. He evidently told David that he could help me, and an appointment was arranged at his office on a Saturday, when the building was all but deserted.

The agent told me of glittering opportunities in Hollywood, but there was one provision. "They always want to look at your legs," he explained. Obligingly, I lowered my underdrawers and he felt my upper thighs, to check muscle tone it could be presumed. That was all that happened. I then pulled my shorts back up. He may have lost his nerve and aborted the project, seeing how innocent I was and knowing that David would almost certainly be told about this. Later I realized that my legs were not what he was interested in, but at the time I only felt that it was rather strange and incongruous. My virginity was left intact. I never told David about it, and went on with my young teenage life as before.

After my experience at the Stony Creek Theater in 1938, almost a year had gone by before I was on a stage again. By the spring of 1939 David Howard and I had become good friends, and he was on now on the phone with a proposition. He knew of a summer stock company in Keene, New Hampshire, which needed a young actor. However, they didn't want to pay him, and so they proposed the following arrangement: The Equity pay scale for junior members was then $25 weekly. This document was signed by me and by Freeman Hammond, the producer and director: "Arthur Anderson agrees to lend Freeman Hammond the sum of $200.00, to be repaid at whatever time and in whatever manner Freeman Hammond may determine." $200, of course, was my total salary for the 8-week season, plus round-trip railroad fare which he was to pay. Another player with the same arrangement was Phyllis Thaxter, slightly older than me, and daughter of the Chief Justice of the Maine Supreme Court, who later went on to a good career in films and on stage. I did not feel victimized. It was something I wanted to do, although I am sure Actors' Equity would have gone up in smoke if they had heard of it. I was by then seventeen and a half years old. And so, on June 23, I got on the train at Grand Central, with my bicycle in the baggage car.

My first role was Henry Aldrich, the lead, in Clifford Goldsmith's *What a Life*. The first day of rehearsal I came down with the worst allergy (it was then called hay fever) I had ever known. It may have come from dust on the train, or different pollens my body was not used to. A doctor in Keene gave me ephedrine sulfate capsules, and the sneezing never came back.

The theater was in a red barn in the foothills of the Monadnock Mountains. It was in a beautiful setting, and ideal for a summer theater. The only trouble I had there was during the first performance week when a huge June bug lodged itself in my shirt and buzzed around frantically during the one emotional scene, when Henry is accused of stealing the band instruments. I was temporarily panicked until I got it out. Afterwards, the actress who played my mother sniffed: "Well! Unprofessional behavior!" I should have liked to have seen her with a huge bug in her bosom.

Most of the actors lived and boarded next door, in the white clapboard Colonial-style house of Mr. and Mrs. Alfred Colony. I could bike into the town of Keene when I was off, and generally experience the New Hampshire countryside. To add to these pleasures a Boston & Maine train would come puffing up the hill behind the Colonys' house every day on its way to Bellows Falls, Vermont.

Playing eight performances a week, while rehearsing next week's play, was valuable experience. I was working at full tilt, and found that learning lines, while always drudgery, became easier with practice, and this ability served me well in the future. Speaking of learning lines, in those days actors were not given scripts of the play but only sides. Sides were each half a page, and contained only your own speeches and the last six or seven words of your cues. By themselves they were gobbledygook. Learning lines this way, out of context, was very difficult until after the first reading of the play with the full cast.

My other mentor, Knowles Entrikin, and his wife had a house in West Brattleboro Vermont nearby, and I was able to visit with him and David, who were working on scripts together. When Keene was over I returned home on Sunday, September 2. The next morning, September 3, I was awakened by the radio playing very loudly. Germany had invaded Poland.

For the next two years my life was again taken up with radio, and school. In May 1941 I graduated from The Professional Children's School. High school had taken me five years because of having to repeat some subjects. PCS graduations were always held in a Broadway theater, and this was The John Golden. My diploma was signed and presented by Mr. Golden himself.

In July 1940 I decided on an adventure that had nothing to do with acting. It was taking a bicycle trip in New England, staying at youth hostels. American Youth Hostels were patterned after European models. Young people after hiking or biking could stay at local farmers' houses for practically nothing. You made your own meals (nothing can equal the taste of fresh, unpasteurized milk, or a melon picked fresh from the garden). You would carry a sleeping sack for the nighttime, and consult an AYH guide book for the location of your next stop.

On July 23 I took my bike off the train at New Haven, Connecticut, and headed north. I rode mostly alone, but there were always interesting people at the next hostel. I had wanted for a long time to see The Flume and The Old Man of the Mountain in New Hampshire. One hostel was in a farmer's house at Lincoln, in Grafton County. After a good sleep I was awakened by a strange sound. It was a herd of cows being driven through the town's main street, which was a dirt road.

That day I headed west and my map told me the road skirted Mount Moosilauke, altitude 4810 feet. What it didn't tell me was that the road was a steady upward climb for over ten miles. It was long after dark when I limped into the next small town, and the telephone operator, whose switchboard was in her living room, told me, through a locked door, how to get to the next hostel, which had a lantern burning in a window to guide me. The whole trip was less than two weeks, and featured lovely sights and mosquito bites, but I resolved to go again as soon as I could.

A less-than-thrilling stage appearance was in New Jersey in November. A producer there planned to bring a little bit of Broadway to Union City, and his first outing was *What a Life*. Rehearsals began November 4 in Manhattan, in an empty floor of an office building — gloomy to say the least. The theater was one that I believe had once presented strippers and burlesque shows, which Mayor LaGuardia had banned from New York City in the 1930s. I was Henry Aldrich again for a week — so different from the lovely barn theater in Keene — but it was work on a stage, and not to be turned down.

I was never aggressive enough in looking for theater work and did not have an agent at that time, but work did come along from an unexpected quarter. In the summer of 1941 I again found myself playing at the Stony Creek Theater, and staying at the venerable Flying Point Hotel, but the atmosphere could not have been more different from the joyful excitement of The Mercury. A new play, *The Good Neighbor*, had been written by Jack Levin, who was in advertising in Baltimore. It was a plea for tolerance and resistance to mob mentality. The leads were an aging Jewish couple who kept a second-hand store. It seemed the Ku Klux Klan was looking for a simple-minded boy named Luther, and the old couple was hiding him in a closet in the store. Gustave Schacht and Anna Appel, both mainstays of the Yiddish theater in New York, were the leads. I was cast as the boy Luther, and there were 15 in the cast. The director was a famous name from a very different quarter, the celebrated novelist Sinclair Lewis. Several of his novels had been made into successful Broadway productions, including *Elmer Gantry, Dodsworth* and *It Can't Happen Here*, but he had never directed a play on Broadway, or indeed anywhere else that I knew of. He was rather tall and lean, had thinning reddish hair, and a rather high, reedy voice.

Mr. Lewis held the first reading in his cottage next to the Flying Point on August 21, and his faithful young assistant, Marcella Powers, was always present. I distinctly remember my first impression of the piece at the reading — that it was a depressing piece of trash. But what did I know, I thought. I was glad to be doing something on stage again.

We opened at Stony Creek September 15 and played there a week. It turned out that after this there would be an out-of-town tryout, then an opening on Broadway. The tryout took place very soon. We played a week in the old red brick Ford's Theater in Baltimore, and then came immediately to New York, where we opened at the Windsor Theater on October 11.

By now I was buoyed up by the momentum of the production, and had begun to think that *The Good Neighbor* was not half bad. That illusion, if not shattered, was partly cracked by the reviews, which were uniformly negative. Lewis Kronenberger, writing for the newspaper *PM*, headlined his review "A Flop Happens Here." Mr. Lewis had interrupted the writing of a novel for which he was under contract to direct the play, and John Anderson wrote in *The Journal-American* that it was not worth interrupting even a haircut.

The second night when I arrived for half hour, I could not help noting that the theater's marquee was dark. That this was not due to a short circuit was confirmed when I came in the stage door and found the company manager, under a work light, paying off the cast. It is easy to say, "Well, that's showbiz," but after weeks of work and devotion by many people to make *The Good Neighbor* a finely tuned success, it had to be, and was, a disappointment.

It was not two weeks later that the disappointment turned to involvement in another project. This was *Little Dark Horse*, starring Walter Slezak and Cecilia Loftus, and produced by Blackwell and Curtis. It was about a French businessman who returns from a long stay in Africa, and brings back with him a little black boy, his son, who gave the play its title. The director was Melville Burke.

What they needed this time was someone who could understudy the older teenage son, and also be assistant stage manager. I was a good choice because I could play a teenager — I was nineteen at the time but looked younger — and at this point was exempt from the draft.

All of us were soon at the DuPont Theater in Wilmington, and staying, of course, at the DuPont Hotel, which is in the same building. My immediate boss was stage manager Cledge Roberts, who had spent enough time as a young leading man on Broadway and elsewhere to be showing a bit of middle age, and now he was a good stage manager. Early on I was learning the technicalities of being an ASM, including giving the actors their calls. Giving the stagehands a call was another matter. The deckhands were sitting on the stage one day when I relayed a message from Cledge that there would be a light rehearsal that afternoon at two o'clock. "Kid," said the head carpenter, "Want to stay out of trouble?" They would not accept anything resembling an order from me, which was a little humiliating, but it was part of my education.

During that brief run I was useful, although I don't remember all of what I did, but at no time was there any mention of rehearsing me in the part I was understudying. That would no doubt come after the New York opening. Meanwhile, if Raymond Roe had been indisposed I would have been expected to go on, which I would have done with script in hand. But it was not a comforting feeling.

Before the New York opening at the John Golden Theater there were last-minute rehearsals, including one which was not on the schedule. Miss Loftus, it turned out, had a problem with drinking, and it was not at all certain that she could perform on opening night. Cledge told me to close the door that led from the backstage hallway to the stage, so that she would not see her understudy being rehearsed when she came in.

This seemed like a simple enough instruction, but, unbelievably, *I could not find the door.* It was camouflaged with fire hoses, ladders and other equipment. Later, Cledge said, "I thought I told you to close that door." I felt stupid. It was like something in a bad dream. I remember the rehearsal went on successfully, and Miss Loftus did make opening night.

Again, the reviews were bad, partly, I think, because the miscegenation involved was distasteful to the critics. The show ran for a week. My only assignment during that time was to sit up in one of the dressing rooms and make a clean copy of the playing script, no doubt for copyright purposes, which I did on my little Remington portable.

Again, a long hiatus from the New York stage, or any other stage. In the fall of 1942 I knew I would be in uniform soon, so decided to take one more Youth Hostel trip, this one to Vermont. I took a train to Danbury, Connecticut, and biked north from there on Route 7. As always, the accommodations varied quite a bit, but I was used to that. I remember once sleeping in the hayloft of a barn on a fragrant, real straw mattress.

I was chagrined by one experience at a farmhouse in Vermont. Arriving at the hostel in mid-afternoon I got into conversation with the householder's little girl, probably aged about ten or eleven. During it I mentioned that I was an actor, and worked on *Let's Pretend.* Her eyes became wide with wonder and she ran out. I heard her calling, "Mama! Mama! Have I got something to tell *YOU!!!*" I did not see the child again during my stay there, and I'm certain that her parents had strictly forbidden her to ever again come in contact with *that actor.*

This time I had a couple of enjoyable nights at Knowles Entrikin's in West Brattleboro before traveling northward. Due to gas rationing I often had the road to myself for long periods. I cycled as far north as Stowe, Vermont, deciding not to go farther because my bike's rear wheel was seizing, and I knew that this was not something that could be corrected with 3-In-One Oil. I came home from Stowe on the train, enjoying in the dining car a good meal and for dessert some wonderful, flaky apple pie, topped with a slice of Vermont cheddar.

I can never claim that my career, or my life for that matter, was routine or humdrum. As long as I had my work, freelance and irregular as it was, life was never discouraging. However, Pearl Harbor had happened and we were now at war.

When I got my draft notice at the beginning of 1943, I didn't have that many personal affairs to wind up, except to notify Nila Mack that I would not be available for *Let's Pretend* for awhile, and she had me do King Feodor in *The Queen Who Couldn't Make Spice Nuts,* which she knew was my favorite *Let's Pretend* role, on Saturday,

January 9. I also got to do a commercial on *Big Sister* that week —
a husband who said, "My wife washes my shirts white as snow with
Rinso."

At age 20 I was still what used to be called a mere stripling. My
professional work was satisfying, but I really lived a very sheltered
life, and needed to branch out and mature. The Army was my chance
to do that.

7
CHAPTER
INTO THE WILD BLUE YONDER
(THREE YEARS, FOUR MONTHS AND THREE DAYS IN THE MILITARY)

When the attack on Pearl Harbor happened in 1941, my eldest brother Edward was 26 years old, George was 24 and I was 19, so it was inevitable that the three Anderson boys would soon be in military service. Edward went first, and was stationed at the US Naval Training Center in Geneva, New York, on the shores of Lake Erie, doing clerical work, for just about the duration of World War II. His wife Lorraine and infant son Edward Jr. went with him. In any case it was sure that I would be next, as my brother George by then had a wife, Gertrude, and four sons, and with so many dependents the military did not call him until much later.

I was eager to do something useful for our country, though not sure what a 20-year-old actor could contribute. I was sworn in January 6 at the Draft Board, which was on the fourth floor of an old loft building at Broadway and 18th Street, and was told to return the next week for my physical. With true patriotic fervor I didn't want to be turned down, and so the night before my physical I ate several bananas so as not to be underweight. Even so, at the huge New York City induction center in Grand Central Palace, as I stood naked on the scales holding only an envelope with my records, the soldier who recorded my weight did a double take, saying to his assistant, "122." Then: *"A hundred and twenty-two??!!"*

On the 13th it was time to report for duty. I said goodbye to my parents in the huge, cavernous space of Pennsylvania Station (since replaced by a concourse that looks like a medium-sized bowling alley). My mother was close to tears, and I was guilty because I felt quite good about this new adventure. The train to

Fort Dix consisted of some of the railroad's oldest cars likely dating from the First World War, which had wooden slat seats.

The Fort Dix Induction Center was a very efficient assembly line where we recruits were issued uniforms, mess kits and duffel bags. My size was instantly determined by a little man who slapped both sides of my mid-section and called out "36 Regular."

We were put in square six-man tents, each with the cast-iron US Army Space Heater No. 1 in the center. It was a cold day in mid-January. After chow we soon loaded the stove with coal, but being New York City boys none of us had ever banked a fire. And so the heater, which had been almost red-hot when Taps were sounded, was by three the next morning stone cold, and so were we — the first shock of my military life.

Four days later a group of us were put on another train, our destination being Atlantic City, for six weeks' basic training. We were now in the US Army Air Force, and were to be quartered in the Marlborough-Blenheim Hotel. The Marlborough Blenheim had been two of the city's older hotels, now combined. The Air Force needed men immediately for ground crew support, and instead of building barracks simply requisitioned every hotel on Atlantic City's Boardwalk. The rooms, which had been luxurious, were now stripped of their carpeting and furniture and each now had six men on Army bunks, and to pass Saturday inspection we had to not only clean every ledge and door lintel, but also scrub the bare cement floor. The only remnants of the hotel's former grandeur were the taps in the bathroom which were labeled *Hot, Cold, Salt* and *Fresh*.

The food was good, and plentiful, always true of stateside posts. Once we had the extra treat of Glenn Miller playing in our mess hall. The hotel's lobby had tall, stately marble pillars. Another of its features was Lieutenant Lamour, who was apparently on loan from the Free French Army. He patrolled the lobby with his baton and in his small cap, his sole duty apparently being to call out every few minutes to us GI's, "DOO NUTT LEAN AGAINST ZE PEELARS!!"

During those six weeks we had close order drill, we had venereal disease lectures, with appropriate posters, one featuring a sultry, cigarette-smoking girl, and the caption was "She may look clean, but. . ." There was always gas mask training. The Germans hadn't used poison gas since World War I, but the Army was taking no chances. We also tramped out to the firing range on a cinder-covered field at Brigantine. Though I hated the scratchy woolen long-john underwear, we really needed our overcoats and every other piece of uniform on those long, cold marches. I qualified on the carbine, a small slightly inaccurate rifle, as well as the M-1, regular size. On rainy days some of our training took place in Convention Hall, which was so huge it had two railroad sidings.

Part of our indoctrination was mechanical aptitude tests. In one of them I was to unscrew some bolts from a nut and then screw them onto another nut, and this was timed by a girl with a stopwatch, who left while I was doing this. She came back shortly and said, "Are you still here?" I had failed, but I didn't let that bother me. Surely the Army would put me into something where I could be useful.

The other occupants of the room on the fourth floor were, of course, New York City boys. I remember only two of them. One apparently had been a Mama's boy, spoiled and unused to any work or discipline. When we reminded him that each of us had to help clean the room for that Saturday's inspection, his reply was a scornful, "Rah, rah, rah."

"Oh yeah?" said another of my roommates. "I'll rah-rah you in the ass."

Another New York City GI was Hanley. Our cultural differences became apparent one day when he said, "Hey, Eannison. Why do you always say 'Teu-uwwssday.' Why dontcha say 'Toosdy' like everybody else?" When I said it would be nice for us to polish our shoes and spruce up for when we'd be free to walk out on the Boardwalk, he said, "For who? For what?" I decided to let it alone.

Something we all hated was Reveille, especially because it was at 4:30 A.M. Corporal Rocco who was the CQ (Charge of Quarters) would patrol the echoing bare cement hallways blowing a particularly strident whistle and shouting, "All right — everybody up! Take your hands off your cocks and pull on your socks! Reveille!" There were, from time to time, also surprise fire drills. The occupants of every hotel had to line up on the boardwalk, in formation, in whatever they had been sleeping in. I remember one man who habitually slept naked was only able to grab a raincoat, not particularly pleasant as the temperatures in Atlantic City were near zero at the time.

My most memorable surprise during basic was the night I was on guard duty in a dimly-lit alleyway. A mysterious black-robed figure appeared. I, in true military fashion, called out, "Halt! Who goes there?" It was only a Salvation Army lassie with coffee and doughnuts. Another Atlantic City adventure was contracting German measles, which the Air Force called "rubella," so as not to give the Germans credit for anything, even a disease. A war-time German spokesman had informed Great Britain that "Ve shall call you ze Bwits." A British spokesman responded with, "Then we shall call you the Germs."

There must have been hundreds of us rubella cases. We were quartered in The Holmhurst, an ancient three-story shingled structure where our main problem was boredom. We were not allowed out, and our only diversion besides mail from home was some dog-eared magazines and putting nickels in a jukebox, but how many times can you listen to even a good song like Gershwin's *Our Love Is Here To Stay?* Both that and The Holmhurst remain in my memory to this day.

When my six weeks' training in Atlantic City was over, in early March, I was part of a group of over a hundred men who were shipping out. *Shipping out* was probably a holdover from the 19th Century, when soldiers were put on ships to travel to their next posts. In World War II if a GI had a cushy job at Headquarters, he was called "permanent party," meaning on the permanent staff at an air base, but if he misbehaved the traditional warning was "shape up or ship out."

We marched over (or probably struggled over, with heavy barracks bags) to an old grubby wrestling arena several blocks from the Boardwalk. This was our assembly point. I was part of a group who were put on a train bound for Omaha, Nebraska. On our arrival we were sent to the aging red brick Rome Hotel in downtown Omaha. There were four of us in Room 131, one flight up from the lobby. The hotel's dining room was now a GI mess hall, and in the lobby was something I had never seen — Soundies. This was the film jukebox promoted by the President's son, Elliott Roosevelt.

Instead of a nickel it cost ten cents, and for your dime you would see whatever number was next on a continuous film loop. One was Fifi D'Orsay singing *I Wanna Be Loved*. Another was a tired, old-fashioned vaudeville sketch involving three Irish working men in which the tag line was, ". . . and when he'd been dead two weeks he looked better than you do now!" This, by the way, was one of the ways that vaudeville performers, ironically, contributed to the end of their own careers. Many vaudevillians were delighted to be asked to make films of their acts, only to find that these films were soon shown in movie theaters, and the screen was on an empty stage.

Though I had flunked my mechanical aptitude test in Atlantic City, I was now assigned to Army Radio School, expected to learn how to build, repair and trouble-shoot problems with Army radios. Every morning we marched in formation up 17th Street, the main drag in downtown Omaha, to the school on Farnum Street. The civilian instructor, Mr. Weinberg, was competent enough, but when asked a question he couldn't answer his reply was always, "We're comin' to that, fellows — we're comin' to that." By the end of the three-month course the man at the workbench next to mine was building a 6-tube superhetrodyne set while I still labored over my more primitive model. One positive was that we had all been promoted to the rank of Corporal — two stripes, and higher pay.

Meanwhile, another soldier and I had inherited girlfriends passed on by men who were shipping out. My girl was Melba Hicks and his was Iris. They both lived at the end of the trolley line where the yellow cars turned around at a tree-lined intersection. We would go to movies and do other things together. There was no sex, but there was kissing and necking, and we had fun, including renting a car one day and driving out to Boys' Town. I had never done much dating, so this was a very important part of my growing up, and a very pleasant interlude in my military life.

I had a strange experience during my Omaha tour of duty. For three or four weeks I found that I was somehow out of myself. I was behaving perfectly normally, but it was as if I were observing myself from outside, what analysts term a *disassociate personality disorder*, which can be emotionally determined. I had suddenly been placed in a life completely different from what I had known, in a different world. Instead of acting in radio studios in Manhattan, I was now subject to a completely different kind of discipline, dealing with a completely different set of places and people. This was not unpleasant, but it was unnerving. Then one Sunday morning while sitting in church everything snapped back into place, and I knew I was myself again. Somehow my brain had made the adjustment.

When radio school was over, a group of us were shipped to Lincoln, the capital of Nebraska, quartered in dorms of The University of Nebraska. We were being interviewed for Army Specialized Training, called ASTP. This was primarily to train engineers for the Army of Occupation after the war's end. I told the officer interviewing me that I really had no talent for being an engineer. After all, I had been an actor in civilian life. "Well, we need some engineers with a sense of humor," he said. He had a quota to fill, and once again, like thousands of civilian soldiers, I was being put into something where I surely didn't fit. Moreover, I had been reduced to the rank of Private.

My next train trip was to Chester, Pennsylvania, and the Pennsylvania Military College, an institution almost as old as West Point. There were still young civilian cadets there who were quartered in Old Main, a large yellow-painted stone building, but they did not interact with the GI's stationed there. I was now part of The 3306th Service Unit, and a group of us soldiers were to be quartered in Dyer Hall. This was an old red brick house probably built about 1901, with a round turret in one corner. Life there was not unpleasant, in spite of the fact that I really didn't feel that I was college material.

I learned to use a slide rule for mathematics, that skill now long forgotten. Math was taught by a lovely old gentleman with white hair, blue eyes and steel-rimmed spectacles who had no doubt come out of retirement to help the war effort. He would begin each hypothesis by saying, "Now, I claim . . ." and then proceed to prove it. He would always begin his summing up with: "Now I think I may safely say without fear of successful contradiction . . ." I will always remember this sentence because it had so many "esses," and every one of them had a semi-liquid sound, probably due to ill-fitting dentures.

There was, of course, continuing military training and also athletics, at which I was not much good. I did enjoy badminton, though, and soccer somewhat. I tried basketball only once: "No, no, Anderson — ya not supposed to run with the ball!" I was somehow able to get out of doing that again. But wherever you were stationed there was always PT — Physical Training, which included calisthenics — mass exercises — sort of exhilarating. I am sure I was never in better physical shape, before or after my years in service.

One negative, though, besides my feeling of being useless at what I was doing, was an infection in my left arm. I had been continuing to get allergy shots for hay fever, which, incidentally, disqualified me from serving overseas. The needle was sterilized by being boiled in a porcelain cooking pot. The arm became infected and had to be lanced.

There were good things about ASTP, though. One was that every other weekend I could get a pass to take a Pennsylvania Railroad train home. Another was that when I notified Nila Mack of my availability she would see that I got a part on *Let's Pretend*, which was now sponsored and paying its actors a lot more than our previous ten dollars a show. I might be a mysterious voice on filter from inside a booth, or something else offstage. Miss Mack felt, rightly, that a soldier in uniform shouldn't be seen onstage on a children's radio program.

By this time I had constructed what I billed as The Only Two-Man Band in Existence. I was both men, of course. A kindly GI had made me a blue-painted box in which was a footboard with bells, electric and manual, mounted on it, and kazoo and train whistle, which I wore around my neck attached to a coat hanger. This, plus my singing and playing the ukulele, was the act. The blue box didn't fit in a barracks bag, of course, so my mother sent it on to me later when I had a more permanent assignment.

The Two-Man Band and I also had the honor of once playing at The Stage Door Canteen. The Canteen, in the basement of the former Nora Bayes Theatre on West 44th Street, provided entertainment and food for thousands of servicemen during the war, and some of our biggest stars served food and washed dishes, while young actresses danced with them.

"War Is Hell" department: (George Spruce and Arthur, off duty)

Back at Chester a more long-lasting upper was my friendship with George Spruce, from Charleston, West Virginia, who also lived in Dyer Hall. He played the upright in the lobby, and we'd sing with that and my uke, always stopping abruptly at 6:30 when it was time to go upstairs and study. His nickname was Bruce Spruce, The Musical Swoose. Another friend was short and blond-haired Irvin Sachritz from Memphis. He was T-Bone, and I was Ack-Ack, because I would do imitations of the Battle of Wake Island — both sides.

The 3306th Service Unit produced a musical variety show at PMC, the cast including soldiers and some of the cadets, which I titled *Gone with the Draft*. There was a barbershop quartet, with one man getting shaved, and a Spring Dance — twelve soldiers in pink paper tutus doing high kicks, and a couple of classical music solos by other talented GI's. I did my imitation of Lew Lehr, the comedian who did movie shorts, and there were good musical numbers by our pick-up orchestra. We had one performance on November 19, 1943, in the PMC gymnasium.

A continuing downer of my time at PMC, besides my infected arm, was the growing feeling that whether I was lazy or just unqualified for higher education, there was no use in my continuing there. It was easy to think of the less lucky GI's who were getting shot at, and dying in Europe and the Pacific. *Don't you realize how lucky you are?*, I asked myself. But that did not change the fact that I was a waste to the taxpayers, and to myself, at good old PMC.

After two terms (six months) had passed I really wanted out of there. Colonel Marion O. French, Regular Army, the commandant, was a gentleman of the Old School — short and ramrod-straight. He was probably delighted to have some grown men to command after years of training boy cadets. I asked for an interview, requested transfer, and after two requests he kindly granted it.

Colonel French and I corresponded after my PMC stint. In a June 1944 letter he told me that all the soldiers had departed in March, and later wrote that "you and other spare men of the Air Force will shortly go to the infantry." I surmise that all of that meant that the Army Specialized Training Program was being discontinued, and if so it was just as well that I got out of it when I did. George Spruce's wife later showed me some beautiful drawings he had made sitting on a hill overlooking a cathedral in Italy, where he was assigned in the Signal Corps. Col. French's last brief Christmas note contained the notation, "I am being retired for disability."

After my stint at Chester I was given a *delay enroute* by which soldiers were given a respite at home before reporting for their next assignment, and I was then ordered to report to Camp Crowder, Missouri. Crowder was a replacement depot, called a *Repple Depple* by GI's. Men were sent there to be classified for permanent assignments, or as permanent as anything ever was in the military. Meanwhile, there were the usual close-order drill, orientation lectures, calisthenics and other time-fillers. Men being taken out to the drill field stood in a huge trailer bus made of plywood, which creaked loudly whenever it moved, The door was in the rear end, and a sergeant would pack us in four at a time, continually intoning "Fo' mo' . . . fo' mo' . . . fo' mo' . . ."

After what must have been another month of uselessness, I was a shipment of one, boarding the train at a lonely flag stop called

McIlheny at about six one morning, one NCO (noncommissioned officer) being assigned to see me off.

My destination was a huge air base at Kearns, Utah, on the outskirts of Salt Lake City. It was there that I experienced a phenomenon that I could only wonder at. It again involved the US Army Space Heater Number 1. A group of us had been doing close-order drill on a huge desolate flat, with only the distant Wasatch Mountains to break the monotony. There was a five-minute break, with the usual permission "Smoke if ya got 'em." It was a sunny day, but quite cold, and a group of us quickly went into an unoccupied barracks, and huddled around the cast iron stove. We held our hands to it, remarking how good it felt. Finally, the whistle blew to fall in, and everybody went back out to the drill field. I was the last to leave, and out of curiosity I opened the lid of the stove. It was cold. It probably had not been lit since the last group shipped out weeks before. I could only smile. My analysis, after long reflection: *The power of suggestion, perhaps?* Or just wishful thinking?

Eventually (exact time periods are not always easy to remember), a group of us were put on a Union Pacific train heading north. Many of us had diarrhea for several days afterward, no doubt from the roast beef we were given in the dining car (lunch was 75 cents), which had a slightly iridescent greenish tinge.

By now I was quite used to train travel, which I had always liked. It was the cheapest and most efficient way for the Army to move large numbers of soldiers. For long distances Pullman sleeping cars were used, but with little hint of luxury. The reason was that one soldier slept in the upper berth, but two of us had to share the lower. Sometimes it was day coaches, all that was available. Most passenger trains were pulled by steam locomotives. On one long trip back East I remember seeing a soldier who couldn't find a seat, and was sleeping soundly on the floor of the vestibule at the end of the car. His face was black with soot from the engine.

On one railroad trip across the Great Plains we stopped at a little nondescript station — North Platte, Nebraska. As soon as the train came to a halt, dozens of GIs raced to the station house, and so did I. There must be something good there, I thought. It was the North Platte Canteen. North Platte was always a twelve-minute stop for the engines to take on water and coal. One of the townspeople had asked the local newspaper why there couldn't be a canteen in the station where soldiers, sailors and Marines could at least get a cup of coffee and a doughnut. This was done. The Union Pacific Railroad donated the space, and a huge network of volunteers came into being, some driving for as much as a hundred miles on their assigned days despite gas rationing, bringing cakes, pies, sandwiches, lemonade, coffee, candy, magazines and other comforts for the servicemen. The canteen was open from five in the morning to past midnight, as a total of fifteen troop trains passed there daily.

The Canteen opened on Christmas night 1941, and finally closed on April 1, 1946. No passenger trains have stopped there for years now, and where the station once stood there is just a little pedestal with a brass marker. The North Platte Canteen was truly the finest example of wartime patriotism and devotion. Bob Green wrote a book about it called *Once Upon a Town*, published by William Morrow.

By now it was March 1944. Our destination was the Army Air Field at Pocatello, Idaho.

Remember the Judy Garland song:

"I Was Born In A Trunk In The Princess Theater In Pocatello, I-da-ho"?

The Princess Theater was indeed in downtown Pocatello. It showed only films now, and had a metal roof which clattered loudly in a rainstorm. Pocatello is in southeast Idaho, bordered by the Wasatch Mountains on the east, and flat desert land on the west. The Army Air Base was at 5,000 feet altitude, and the air was pure, invigorating and carried the piney fragrance of sagebrush. Having had Air Force basic training, I was finally assigned to a real air field — with planes!

The Air Force in those days was known as "the country club of the Army." Life there was supposed to be easier, clean and less hazardous, unless you were in a combat crew, of course. Promotions of officers were supposed to happen very quickly. As evidence of that, the following story: There was a formation of fighter planes with student pilots. Each time the flight commander gave an order to change course or altitude they all acknowledged promptly with the usual "Roger" or "Roger, willco," except for one pilot who always said, "Rodger dodger, you old codger." The flight commander had

had enough of this and said, "Let's cut out that 'old codger' stuff. I'm commanding this flight, and I'm a major." Back came the reply: "Roger dodger, you old codger. I'm a major, too."

Pilots were being trained at Pocatello to fly P-47 single-engine fighter planes built by Republic Aviation. I was relieved that I was not being expected to do radio repairs or troubleshooting, at which I would have been completely useless. What I could and did do was get in the cockpit of each plane I was assigned to, and call the control tower on the P-522 radio, which had several channels which the pilot could change by pushing a button. This produced a loud, ratcheting sound. I would announce the number of the aircraft and ask, "How do you read me?" I'd then check off the results on a clipboard, and go to the next plane. This was not particularly demanding work, but at least I felt that I was doing something useful. It did get boring on one occasion, however, and instead of announcing the plane's number I pressed the transmitter button and said, "Ah, Japanese bomber heah, ah, request-o permission to, ah, wand at, ah, Pocatewwo Air Base. Ovah." The control tower did not reply. If they had I would probably have been court-martialed.

A standing joke on the flight line was that most of us GI radio repairmen were there merely to clean bird shit off the antennas. The skilled work was done mostly by a very capable civilian who also no doubt had the keys to the secret room where . . . hush-hush . . . RADAR was stored. Evenings he would repair civilians' radios in his own shop in downtown Pocatello.

During all of my Army service my parents were faithful correspondents, my mother addressing me as *Dearest Puss*. Most of the news was family news, but I did get a strong indication of life on the home front in a postcard from my father, dated November 19, 1944. He had just had his first Sunday off from the Mack Truck Company in a year, he said. Moreover, 50 soldiers from Camp Kilmer were working at Mack on the night shift. The Mack Truck Company, of course, made heavy equipment for the military. My father was Plant Engineer. He was an expert on heat exchange and compressed air, and his work was intimately connected with The Allies winning the war. Mine, when I thought about it, was not. I really had a leisurely schedule, and the greatest hardship was an occasional stint on night K.P. The only saving grace that I could think of was that I was releasing another man for more important work overseas.

And now back to the War Front: Thursday evening at 9:30 PM *Pass in Review* was broadcast from the enlisted men's service club on the local NBC affiliate KSEI (for Southeast Idaho). It was a mixture of music, commentary and sometimes lame comedy material. Sergeant Don Perkins was writer, director and announcer. After I told Don that I was an actor, I was given lines in the show, and from then on was on every week. Eventually, Don was given orders to ship out. Capt. Ben Rogers, the Public Relations officer, took me off the flight line and put me in charge of the show. More important, he got my MOS (Military Occupation Specialty) number changed to 274, which meant Public Relations Specialist, as of June 24, 1944. Now I could do something I was good at. Public relations, after all, involved civilians' morale, and support for what we were doing at the Air Base. I was in Pocatello, nicknamed Poka-Ta-Hell-Hole by some cynics, for nine months — longer than at any other post in my three years.

The Army was truly a learning experience, if not always a pleasant one. In the barracks I learned to live with men of completely different backgrounds and attitudes, and interestingly with different speech patterns. All these I got used to, except for some of the young men from the mountains of Kentucky and West Virginia. The mountain speech I could never completely understand.

The people in the Public Relations office were pleasant and easy to get along with. Captain Rogers was eventually replaced by Lt. Walter Van Buren, and Cpl. John Moe joined us later. As John Larson he later became a Broadway casting director. A local girl, Nathel Lewis, capably handled a thousand details. The guys in the band, led by Sgt. Joe Konkoly, were a relaxed sort of bunch, and apparently did not do anything strenuous when not performing.

One of Public Relations' functions was to do stage shows promoting War Bond sales. These we did in various small Idaho towns. We soldiers traveled in a recon (a rugged Army version of a station wagon). There was Eric Saline, piano, Russ Thomas guitar, Eddie Menekin who played classical violin, and me. I was the MC, told jokes, played the ukulele, and later did serious pitches to ask the audience to buy United States War Bonds.

We traveled north to one town whose electricity was provided by a diesel generator, and its only connection to the outside world was a single telephone wire. Deer bounded across the road in front of us. Our lodging that night was in the Grubb Hotel, and heat was provided by the flue pipe of the stove in the lobby below, which passed through the center of our room. I did, and do, appreciate how lucky I was to go on these jaunts, see the wild Idaho mountain country and the small towns.

My only close friend at Pocatello was Pfc. Russell Jehn from Union City, New Jersey. We found that we had a lot in common, as we both loved music. I later found that Russ was a great guitarist, and I, of course, loved the uke. I was able to use him in some of the sketches I wrote for the radio program, and we resolved we'd get together after we were discharged.

Benny Coronado, though not a close friend, was unforgettable. He was, I believe, from New Mexico. He was a large man, with dark skin and hawk-nosed Navajo features. I asked him what his civilian occupation was and he replied, "Oh, fucking people." He had, he told me, gotten into some trouble with the law, and was notified by the FBI that it was either prison or enlisting the next day. He chose the latter. He would bring his Army buddies to an after-hours poker game in downtown Pocatello, to which civilians were also invited. As the evening wore on his GI friends would leave one by one, and Benny would start to operate, apparently never being challenged. In the barracks most of us played blackjack — ten cents a hand.

One thing common to all GI's was, of course, profanity. Growing up in radio had broadened my education, as explained earlier, but nothing like the military. Most of the language related to the pelvic area, and was part of the GIs' folklore. The well-known "f" word was, of course, heard constantly. Because of my more or less sheltered life I was at first shocked by it, then accepted it as a part of ordinary conversation. "Fuck" was used as a verb, an adverb, an adjective, a noun and an expletive.

There are many versions of how the word originated, each supposed to be the true one. The most believable to me is that it was used on London police blotters from the 16th Century. *For unlawful carnal knowledge* was the charge written down. It was apparently needed so frequently that it became too much bother for the constable to write all that down, and hence the short, four-letter acronym became standard.

The word became part of military shorthand during World War II. That was when SNAFU was invented, SNAFU, of course, meaning *situation normal — all fucked up*. A variation soon appeared: TARFU: *Things are really fucked up*. The ultimate came a little later in the war, capping it creatively, I thought: "FUBAR," which means *fucked up beyond all recognition*.

The only time I remember "fuck" being used at all creatively was by one of the Southern mountain man in our barracks. Describing an acquaintance who was less than ambitious, he said that the man spent most of his time "jes' fuckin' the dawg, fuckin' the dawg." Whether this exotic practice was actually indulged in or not, it was a good metaphor for a useless or non-productive occupation.

"Shit," of course, was used almost as frequently. Like the other word, it became not so much a profanity as an ordinary form of expression. Only twice did I hear it used with any originality. One was when I overheard a GI who was frustrated that something had gone terribly wrong say, "Shit, fuck, piss and corruption." The other was a variation of the ordinary, derisive "Aw, you're fulla shit," heard dozens of times a day. Again, it was spoken by one of the mountain men in the barracks, who said, "Man, you as full of shit as a tree is of owls."

I cannot resist one more story about the US Army Space Heater Number 1. Each man would take turns bringing in buckets of coal from the wooden bunker outside the barracks, to keep one of the three stoves going. If no one did, we would all be cold that night. The fuel was soft coal, the lowest grade, which was okay if you stoked the fire correctly. It had a slightly sweet, acrid odor. It was a cold Sunday afternoon. Some of us were sitting around the barracks. One of my bunkmates had put a huge lump in the stove an hour before, and it looked as if this had choked the fire and put it out. After half an hour the pent-up gasses from the soft coal exploded, "WHOOMP!!," sending the lid flying open with a loud clank, and depositing soot all over. The stove survived the blast, and provided all of us with a good laugh.

The fighter planes were, of course, what the air base was all about. You could hear engines being revved up all day and all night.

It was a constant roar which after awhile you didn't notice. One evening while sitting in the barracks I heard a sound as if someone had dropped a heavy book on the floor. I instinctively knew what it was. A pilot trainee had been banking for a turn and did not have enough air speed. The plane slid off to one side and he was killed.

The radio program was discontinued in late 1944, as the flight training was winding down. Then I was shuttled to various spots in Texas — first Greenville, which is near Dallas, then Avenger Field in Sweetwater, where another enlisted man and I were the entire public relations department. The only memorable part of that tour of duty for me was that I was back on the air. Station KXOX in Sweetwater needed a Sunday afternoon disc jockey, and it was my job to run the board, play records, do commercials and keep the log. Again, I felt very lucky. The pay was 80 cents an hour.

I had spent V-E Day in Sweetwater and on V-J Day was confined to the base in Spokane, Washington. And now here I was, with steel helmet and rifle, boarding a troop ship in Los Angeles bound for Hawaii, to replace a man who had earned discharge points in the combat zone. Again, it was treading water. Somehow I was kept semi-busy at Kahuku Air Base on the north side of Oahu, preparing weekly orientation lectures for the troops, to keep them up on current affairs. I also had the onerous job of driving a jeep into Honolulu weekly to pick up and return training films to be shown in the base theater. This was my last tour of duty before being put on a troop ship which took us across the Pacific, under the Golden Gate Bridge, and then docked at Richmond, California. Then one more Pullman (two men in the lower berth again) and back to Fort Dix, where my adventure had begun. Finally, on Saturday February 16, 1945, I was told that I could leave the next day with my Honorable Discharge. Moreover, some kind-hearted officer had promoted me to Sergeant.

That afternoon some of us were sitting around the barracks — too early for chow — when Retreat was sounded. Retreat is the official end of the day's duties, when you stand at attention and salute as the American flag is lowered, and a bugle sounds the traditional call. There was no order to fall in, but a few of us wanted to, including me. After three years of what I thought was mostly wasted time, I was still proud to have been a small part of what some people say was this country's last just war. The skinny 122-pound draftee was now three years older, weighed 135, and was also presumably somewhat more mature.

It is difficult to describe the mixture of pride and nostalgia I felt as I saluted for the last time. The next morning my brother George showed up in his Mercury convertible and drove me back to 335 West 14th Street.

8
CHAPTER
LOOKING FOR WORK

Any actor who is able to get sufficient work to actually make a living in the profession is called a Working Actor, which is what I have been for most of my career. Just out of uniform after being away for over three years, however, I faced a totally unknown future — not scary — I am basically an optimist — just unknown.

I was immediately welcomed back to *Let's Pretend* by Nila Mack. The program was now sponsored by Cream of Wheat, so the pay was quite respectable. There was also security in knowing that I'd probably have that for some time to come, as well as other radio programs I'd previously been called for. I had done very well in radio since the age of twelve, and there was no reason to think that this would not continue. Also, I still lived with my parents on West 14th Street, so there was no immediate worry about the cost of living. All of these good things, though, posed a serious problem. To put it simply, as one of the witches says in *Macbeth*, "For you all know, security is mortals' chiefest enemy." In short, I was not hungry enough to commit to a career as a serious actor. Of course, I did not think of it that way. I just took what life offered. I did know that I wanted to continue in theater, though, and so I had to learn a skill with which I was completely unfamiliar — *Making the Rounds*.

In the 1940s this, of course, meant literally walking from one producer's office to the next, asking, "Anything for me today?" Theatrical producers then still had casting offices where actors were seen. The ones that come most quickly to mind are those of John Golden, Brock Pemberton and The Shuberts. It was wearisome work, and highly uncertain.

I slowly learned that there were ways to get help, though. You could always read *Variety* (15 cents a copy) to see who was casting, and there were telephone calls and letters, but unless you had an agent the best way was to go there, hoping that if you couldn't see the producer there was someone in that office who might know you, or if not might think that you were just what the producer was looking for. You might also meet friends there who would have other information on who was casting, or soon would be. Now we call it Networking.

I remember one day in a producer's outer office there were a bunch of us sitting around on benches waiting for The Great Man to appear, possibly scan the crowd and say, "Oh, yes! I want *you* to stay." (This practically never happened, of course, but we waited anyway.) On this occasion he did emerge, but accompanied by a middle-aged actor who was full of himself, and who wore an overcoat over his shoulder, a la John Barrymore, saying to the producer in resonant tones, I have always thought for our benefit: "Well, I think it's maahhvelous — simply maahvelous!"

Beginning in the middle 1940s there was also another job-hunting site which I hadn't even known about — Walgreen's Drug Store, on the corner of Broadway and 45th Street. For a nickel you could buy a cup of coffee or a lemon coke. In the basement was a bank of pay telephones, and on Wednesdays an intense young man named Leo Shull would appear there, with his mimeographed newsletter called *Actors' Cues*, which he sold for a quarter. It had the latest information on who was presumably casting and sometimes what the roles were, with phone numbers and addresses. These were sometimes incorrect and turned out to be in the middle of the East River. But that made no difference. Actors would immediately rush to the phones trying to reach a producer's or an agent's office. No one knew where Leo Shull got this information, and jokes were made about how unreliable it could be.

Whatever sloppy editing there was in *Actors' Cues*, however, there was enough *right* information that the paper did very well, eventually reaching a printed format, with paid ads, and renamed *Showbusiness*. It is now under new management, and Leo Shull is long gone, but he was a pioneer in getting useful information to performers. *Backstage*, founded in 1960, has East Coast and West Coast

A composite.

editions, and also publishes *Ross Reports*, a useful casting guide for all entertainment media.

The first thing I needed after getting out of service was pictures, and knew I needed a theatrical photographer, quite different from a *portrait* photographer, whose work you might find on your aunt's piano. I must have used a dozen or more over the years, but in every case I tried to find shots that would show what roles Arthur Anderson *the actor* might be able to play. There'd always be serious ones for

Call REGISTRY *For*

ARTHUR ANDERSON

VOICE RANGE: 18-28.

TYPE OF WORK: Juvenile leads, young characters.

DIALECTS: English, Irish, Tough, Southern.

STAGE: 4 B'way plays including Orson Welles' Caesar and Shoemakers' Holiday. Summer stock (including leads), ELT shows.

TELEVISION: NBC.

RADIO: 12 years N. Y. Currently: Lawyer Dan Tucker (Mark), Let's Pretend (9th yr.), School of the Air (9th yr.). Also This Is Your FBI, The Shadow, Aunt Jenny, Big Sister, David Harum, CBS Workshop, Cavalcade, Orson Wells. Transcriptions.

LA 4-1200

A radio casting card.

dramatic roles and smiling shots for comedy. They are still called 8X10 glossies, ready to whip out of your briefcase at appointments or put in the mail.

Especially for work in commercials I'd also have another set of pictures called *composites* — different Arthur Andersons; all humorous ones (see illustration). Over the years these have been phased out, and are now used only for print work.

The haphazard world of looking for jobs became a little more organized in 1944, when a young actress named Terese Hayden started *Players' Guide*, with the blessing if not the sponsorship of Actors' Equity. Each performer's listing carried a small photo, with credits, agent's name if any, and phone number. Started in softcover, it eventually became a hard-bound book, printed on good paper, and separated into categories including *Leading Men, Leading Ladies, Ingénues, Character Actors, Comedians* and *Children*. If you were a member of a performers' union you brought your photograph, credits and your money to Terry's office, which you reached by climbing two flights in the brownstone row house on West 47th Street where Equity was located. And when the Guide came out three months later, you were *identified*.

My first listing for which I have a record was in the 1949 edition. It included my Mercury Theatre credits, of course, Aaron Copland's

Second Hurricane, radio and television credits, my home phone and my message service.

As *Players' Guide* grew, an actor named Paul Ross took over. He and his wife did a rushing business once a year and the book became larger, heavier and more important. It was distributed free to agents, producers and others who could hire performers. Finally, in 1996, the printed edition was discontinued. Fewer casting people wanted to handle a heavy volume, and they could now view actors' credits online. But the book had been invaluable to me, and to literally thousands of us performers in advancing our careers.

Making rounds in radio was simpler, but just as necessary, and the basic insecurity of a freelance actor was no different — just the medium. Actors would mail 3X5 cards, printed with their radio credits and the name of their message service. But just as often contacts to directors and casting people would be made by telephone. "Oh, hello. This is Joe Smith. I heard you needed a villain on the show next week. Well (doing a villainous laugh), I'm one of the most truly villainous people you'll find". . . . or some other truly witty, sincere, or charming way to say "anything for me today?," depending on who you were and what was being cast.

After I got out of uniform I sent blotters to directors. Ballpoint pens had not yet been invented. There were still wartime clothing shortages, and my message was:

WHITE SHIRTS — YOU CAN'T GET 'EM!!
BUT I'M BACK!!!
(WITH MY PICTURE AND PHONE NUMBER.)

Another ploy was the *Gag of the Month*, put out by Eddie Wragge and another actor. One month every radio director and casting person got a small cactus with a little tag attached: "I'M STICKING YOU FOR A JOB." Undignified and even cheap though some of these were, they got attention in the very competitive world of radio.

In live television, casting was done by many production companies such as David Susskind's Talent Associates, and, of course, by the networks (Eleanor Kilgallen at CBS and Bill Kaufman at NBC). There was also an affable middle-aged man called Captain Anderson at NBC, who interviewed actors, but I never heard of his actually doing any casting, except occasionally for extras. Actors trooped to his office at 1270 6th Avenue, signed in and left, feeling that they had done something useful. Performers also did auditions for him in an unoccupied radio studio at 30 Rockefeller Plaza. And each of us would think, *Well, you never know . . .*

The most persistent and organized round-maker I ever knew was an actor named Jay Barney. He scheduled fifteen minutes every Wednesday morning to read *Variety* (for free, of course) in the Equity lounge. He made his rounds not on foot but by motor scooter. I understand that at one time he had two motor scooters — one in New York and one in Hollywood. Actors' Equity in the 1940s still held its membership meetings in the Main Ballroom of the Astor Hotel. At one meeting there was an intermission so that those present could cast their ballots for a Council election. During this pause I heard a persistent "ticka-ticka-tick" coming from the front row. It was Jay, not wasting a minute. He had his little portable on his knee and was typing postcards to casting directors. Other actors used to make fun of Jay's routines, but I think that was partly out of envy, because none of them were able to equal his organization and commitment.

Jay Barney was particularly devoted to a better lot for performers, and proved it by serving faithfully for 12 years on the Equity Council.

There were, and still are I am sure, clever ploys by actors to get noticed by casting people. One actor showed up at the office of an ABC casting director announcing that he was a delivery man for a bakery. He was admitted to her office even though she hadn't ordered anything. He then opened a box on her desk, which contained a large strawberry sheet cake, with his picture and phone number on top.

My only original ploy was when Parsonnet Films was casting a comedy for which I was interviewed — the role of a country bumpkin. I showed up at their Times Square office in my usual jacket, shirt and tie, and after I read I could tell that they were unimpressed. So I went around the corner where I knew there was a coin-in-the-slot photo machine, and for a quarter I took four pictures of myself with tie off, hair disheveled, and wearing an idiotic expression. I sent this into the casting director's office, and got the job.

Physically making rounds has been unknown for some years now. I could tell that the territory was changing in the 1960s when I found agents' doors locked and notices outside that read:

DO NOT KNOCK. DO NOT RING. SLIDE PICTURE AND RESUME UNDER DOOR.

And now, of course, you can't even get past the building's guard in the lobby unless you are on a list of people who have appointments.

An actor's life is, of course, more bearable if he or she has an agent. Many articles have been written on *How to Get an Agent*, a subject which I will not attempt to go into. In my postwar acting career there were many agents I respected, some of whom I (and everybody) was in awe of, and a few I liked. One of my first contacts after the Mercury was William Liebling. Bill Liebling was a small, intense, and I thought brilliant man. Right after *Julius Caesar* closed I visited him at his office in the RCA Building. When he heard I'd been working for Orson Welles, he at once told his secretary, "Get me Orson Welles." "Orson Welles? Himself? In person?" she said. I laughed inwardly because I knew that Orson just did not answer telephones.

Another agent I knew in those postwar years was Lucille Phillips. She helped me get my Screen Actors' Guild card in 1950 by telling the union that at the time there was no one else available. I was a member of the audience applauding Jane Pickens as she sang, in a short for Paramount Pictures. And though the job was as an extra, the card itself was an important entrée. Max Richards, at 1776 Broadway, was one whose office I'd visit often, and wait, and wait, and wait. Ironically, it was years later when I said to myself, "The hell with this" and did not go there anymore, that I started getting calls, and occasionally jobs through the Richards office.

Then there were Chamberlain and Lyman Brown. They were in a building on West 45th Street. On the ground floor was a beauty parlor, and the sickly sweet smell of wave-setting lotion permeated not only that business, but filtered up to the Browns' office on the third floor. They would contact actors to come for appointments by means of typewritten penny postcards, a great money-saver over telephone calls.

The reception room walls were completely covered with posters of shows they'd cast on the Subway Circuit (theaters in the Bronx and Coney Island), yellowing newspaper reviews and 8 X 10 pictures of actors they'd booked, some very well known.

At the top of the theatrical line was Jane Broder. She was known as formidable and practically unseeable, if there is such a word. My wife Alice in her acting days went one day to Miss Broder's office in the triangular Times Building in Times Square. The door was ajar, and as she put her hand on the knob a voice from inside boomed: "DO I KNOW YOU???... GET OUT!!"

The gentleman agents I remember included Stephen Draper on 57th Street and Johnson Briscoe of Briscoe & Goldsmith, who had an office at 522 5th Avenue. There is still an impressive clock on a 30-foot pedestal on the sidewalk at that address. A Southern gentleman from Georgia was Michael Thomas. Fresh from The University of The South (Sewanee), he came to New York to launch an acting career. He did some work in live TV, and I first met him in 1957 when we were both playing in the National Company of *Auntie Mame*, which starred Constance Bennett. In 1966 Michael decided he belonged in the business end of the theater, and became a very successful agent. This lasted for more than 30 years. In 1998 he decided that perceptions were changing, and it was time to phase out when he received a casting breakdown with the following description: *She is 26 years old, but still agile.*

Michael and I have many friends in common, and keep in touch to this day.

An important goal in every actor's career is to get an audition — actually reading for whoever is casting — a consummation devoutly to be wished. Theater auditions I succeeded in getting in the '40s usually took place on the empty stage of a theater, lit only by a glaring work light that was called the "ghost light." I would have a script, of course, and do the scene with a stage manager, who in most cases could not really read lines but just give cues, but it was my task, of course, to give something approximating a performance. Then one of the invisible voices sitting in the orchestra would either give a suggestion for doing the scene again, or say, "Thank you. We'll let you know." This could be either a sign that they hadn't made up their minds yet — or a sign that they had. In any event, I would tell myself not to worry about it — I'd done the best I could — and go on to whatever might come next.

Roddy McDowall had a perfect technique for handling the nervousness of auditions. He would go on the empty stage with the following take: "These people out front are renting this theater from me . . . and they're behind in the rent."

Producers and directors usually show great consideration for an auditioning actor, who they know is in a very insecure position. The British actor-manager Herbert Beerbohm Tree did no such thing. He had no patience with ineptitude. In 1908 a young actor chose a speech from *Macbeth* for his audition, coming out on stage and saying,

> Is this a dajjer which I see before me,
> the handle toward my hand?

Mr. Tree told the stage manager, "I'm not sure I heard correctly. Would you ask the young man to do the speech again?"

> "Is this a dajjer which I see . . ."
> "Throw that bujjer out," said Tree.

Of tremendous help to my career and to those of many others was the Equity Library Theatre, started in 1943 by actor Sam Jaffe, by Actors' Equity and George Freedley, curator of the New York Public Library Theatre Collection. It was known as ELT. Performances were originally in public libraries, then in ELT's own theater at Lenox Hill Playhouse and later at Masters Institute on West 103rd Street. I did three ELT productions, *The White Devil* in a library on 181st Street shortly after my discharge, Monsieur Martin in *Hotel Paradiso* at Lenox Hill, then several roles in *A Thurber Carnival* at Masters. There was no admission charge, and agents and casting people received special seating. But being on a stage before an audience was always a joy, and was an invaluable experience whether or not that production led directly to a job. ELT lasted for 47 years, then closed in 1990 due to lack of funding.

Hundreds of careers, including mine, were greatly helped by The American Theatre Wing. In World War II the British War Relief

Society was invaluable in helping UK servicemen, sending every-thing from knitted woolen mittens to boxes of cookies, and before Pearl Harbor, while this country was still neutral, an American Theatre Wing of the Society was started by theater people here who were sympathetic to the British cause. Now, of course, it is simply The American Theatre Wing, and has for some years presented the Tony Awards for theatrical excellence. An American serviceman, red-headed Winston O'Keefe, who was in the US Army Tank Corps, had the idea of helping newly discharged performers who were eligible for college training under the GI Bill of Rights, but who would rather get back to theatrical work than go to college. His idea was a Professional Training Program, which would help them reinforce their theatrical skills — an ingenious idea for which the Theatre Wing was naturally suited. There was a former Greek Orthodox church at 432 West 44th Street just west of 9th Avenue, an old red brick building which was available, and this became the program's headquarters. I was one of those who couldn't care less about college, my Army college experience in 1943 having been a complete bust anyway, and so I enthusiastically enrolled.

The courses I took at the Theatre Wing included *Acting* with Joseph Anthony, *Makeup* with Herman Buchman, *Stage Management, Body Movement* with Lucas Hoving, *Piano* with Charles Kingsley, and *Singing* with George Rasely. There were also lectures by people important in the theater from whom all of us learned a lot. Mr. Rasely would sit in a wooden armchair with a smile on his face, cigar in hand, which I never saw him smoke, and sing the most beautiful, effortless high notes, with perfect diaphragm support.

Radio, which employed many actors, was not neglected either. Some of the top directors had us performing and recording programs, another way of learning, and a few of us got radio jobs as a result. The head of the radio division was Arthur Hanna, busy director of many daytime serials and nighttime programs. As all of the Wing students were men, volunteer actresses were also recruited, and this helped some of them get jobs, too.

The American Theatre Wing also had direct employment results for me. There were performances of scenes from plays at the Greek church, with audiences of directors, agents and casting people. One of my performances was a scene from the play *June Moon* by Ring

Lardner. It takes place in a Pullman compartment. It is the wedding night of a young couple who don't have the foggiest idea of what to do, and their embarrassment and self-consciousness is both painful and hilarious. From this came many weeks' work for Gerald Savory in summer stock at the Westchester Playhouse in Mt, Kisco, N.Y., as well as many weeks in winter stock for Harry Young at the Playhouse in Albany N.Y.

I like to think that one day I got one of my most valuable lessons in acting at the Theatre Wing — worth almost as much as all the other courses. Marc Daniels, later an important television director (*I Love Lucy* and other shows) was directing me in a scene from *Abe Lincoln in Illinois*. I was given the role of an old man. Probably self-conscious about being twenty-three years old and doing an octogenarian, I resorted to the usual clichés — quavering voice, shuffling step, bent posture and all the rest. In the middle of the scene, Marc stopped the rehearsal and barked, "ARTHUR!! STOP ACTING!!"

The message was, don't play labels. Don't play results. Play the play. Quavering voice and shuffling step can come later, if at all. I cannot claim that I have remembered that for every role, every rehearsal for the rest of my career. But I have tried to, and I know it has helped. Thank you, Marc Daniels.

In looking for work, the full-time occupation of most actors, I've had invaluable help in many places and from many people. As for Making the Rounds, every actor is always doing that, even if only mentally. Though my own aggressiveness has not always been as strong as it could have been, work has always come along, and that has sustained me for 72 years.

9
CHAPTER
GETTING WORK

I have done so many kinds of acting in so many places that telling it chronologically — ". . . And then I did . . ." — would be as dull as a songwriter's ". . . And then I wrote . . . ." Anyway, now that I was a civilian again not much happened immediately work-wise, except *Let's Pretend, American School of the Air* and some other live radio shows.

One of them, for which I was frequently called until it disappeared in 1956, was *Aunt Jenny's Real Life Stories*, on which I frequently got to play troubled teenagers, ". . . sponsored by Spry, the all-vegetable shortening." On this fifteen-minute daytime show Aunt Jenny (Edith Spencer) would spin a yarn for Dan Seymour, the announcer, supposedly in her kitchen. Each story had an entirely different cast, and was wrapped up in five episodes. Dan frequently got to try some of her cooking and baking, made, of course, with the sponsor's product. Another bit of folksiness was her canary, occasionally whistled by Henry Boyd who I knew from *Let's Pretend*.

In November 1946, I was on a broadcast of *This Is Your F.B.I.*, directed by Jerry Devine, which we did in a hotel ballroom in Atlantic City. If memory serves, the sponsor, the Equitable Life Assurance Society, was holding its annual stockholders' meeting there, and what could be more logical than showing off their radio program of which they were so proud. Whether I was playing a good guy, a bad guy or an innocent victim, I don't remember, but it was a strange feeling to be back in the city where I'd been in an entirely different world only three years before, in Army basic training.

David Howard.

Knowles Entrikin was now working for the Ruthrauff & Ryan ad agency, the same one that presented *Aunt Jenny.* Knowles called one day in February to ask my plans for the summer. I told him I was going on another bicycle trip, this time to the Gaspe Peninsula. "No, you're not," he said. "You're going to be on a summer radio series." Knowles was to direct *Lawyer Tucker*, a CBS Thursday night show about a shrewd but warm-hearted small-town attorney, to be played by Parker Fennelly. Amos Tucker's law partner was to be Maurice Wells, and their slightly sharp-tongued housekeeper was Mae Shults. I was cast as Mark, a well-meaning teenager who had previously served time for a crime it turned out he did not commit. The authors were Howard Breslin, who later became a good friend, and none other than David B. Howard. My network of loving friends had come through again. Knowles and Parker had known each other in live theater since long before Titus Moody or *Allen's Alley* were thought of.

Since Mark was to be a running part, meaning regularly on the show, there had to be an understanding about money. "What do you want?" said Knowles. I immediately replied, "A hundred dollars and billing." Since union scale was then about seventy-five this was not unreasonable, nor was including my name in cast credits. David and Howie alternated writing scripts, and whoever's name was mentioned first by Don Hancock, the announcer, was the one who'd written that week's episode. We did 13 broadcasts of *Lawyer Tucker* that summer. There was an orchestra conducted by John Gart. The sponsor was Auto-Lite Spark Plugs. The scripts were humorous and well written, and this was better than The Gaspe.

Meanwhile, *Let's Pretend* was at its height, sponsored by Cream of Wheat on the entire CBS network, and better known than ever before. And so Columbia Records decided to produce *Pretend* record albums, again directed by Nila Mack, and the five-man ensemble directed by Maurice Brown was now a full orchestra, with brass, reeds and tympani. The records were 78 rpm ten-inchers (long-playing records were still years away), three in each album, and each side being three-and-a-half minutes long. That gave us 21 minutes for each story, about the same as on the broadcast, because there were no commercials, and Brownie wrote a short musical "button" at the end of each side. I had roles in all of them, including the wicked Giant in *Jack and the Beanstalk*, and The Ogre in *Puss in Boots*.

The Theatre Wing showcase was now beginning to show results. The first call came in November 1948 from Marc Daniels who had been one of my instructors there. He was directing a Christmas script, "Joy to the World," on *The Ford Television Theatre*. It starred

Eddie Albert, and I was Floyd, the office boy (still not quite out of teenage parts).

The show was telecast by CBS from Grand Central Station, which sounds like an unlikely place to do television. However, several floors above what was then the main waiting room there are large spaces with high ceilings and no columns. They were ideal for studios, and in midtown Manhattan at that. This was my television network debut.

Coaxial cables now reached from coast to coast, and advertisers were beginning to sign on to the new medium. Soon after that, TV programs could now be recorded on videotape, vastly better than kinescopes, which had been done by photographing the images on a video screen, and resulted in grainy and murky pictures.

Most of the Theatre Wing ex-GIs were interested in stage work, and the Wing turned out to be a blessing for me in that department. Gerald Savory called me first in 1949 for *The Winslow Boy* at the Westchester Playhouse in Mt. Kisco, N.Y. The Playhouse was on the grounds of Lawrence Farms, formerly a big estate, now broken up into suburban plots. The theater was a stucco-covered barn on Route 117, between Mt. Kisco and Chappaqua. It could not have seated more than 300, but it was an Equity company, and playing there was a great satisfaction. The weeks I was playing there, most of us stayed at Effie Phyffe's house nearby, and ate at Andy's Tavern.

In 1949 I was also Freddie Eynesford-Hill in Shaw's *Pygmalion*, Prof. Higgins being played by Gene Lyons, and Lee Grant was a delightful Eliza. In 1950 we did *Brother Rat*, and Tom Drake was the star. By then there had been several changes at The Westchester Playhouse. Effie Phyffe was no longer taking in roomers, and the actors had to make do with other accommodations. During the *Brother Rat* engagement I was quartered at someone's estate in the elegant town of Bedford, New York. Another actor and I slept in a summer house on the grounds, which was all right except that the family had a pet rabbit which was quartered with us, and which left small pellets on the furniture from time to time. A nice interlude, though, was provided by one of the apprentices whose family had a large in-ground pool, and a couple of swims there that week were fun and relaxing.

I guess my biggest role at The Westchester Playhouse was Pulver in *Mister Roberts*, directed by Ed Binns, who also played Doc. I remember two things most vividly from that show. First, the quick change I had to make after the explosion, into my dress uniform for the next scene. I had to strip almost naked in the theater's basement for that one, obligingly helped by three of the apprentices, or apprenti as actors jokingly called them. The other memory was not a happy one. After the hectic opening night I was exhausted, and refreshed myself with a punch made of Orange Crush and gin. It was a hot night, and I drank several glasses, resulting in a colossal hangover. The next day was a matinee, and my parents had come up to see the show. Sharing lunch with them at Andy's, I almost lost it when hot buttered toast was brought in.

My most memorable experience at Mt. Kisco was playing Tenpin (the hero's best friend) in Kurt Weill and Maxwell Anderson's *Knickerbocker Holiday.* It starred Burl Ives as Peter Stuyvesant, the villainous one-legged Governor of New Amsterdam, supported by Betty Oakes and Warde Donovan as the romantic leads, and Morley Meredith as Washington Irving. Delightful character actors Will Kuluva and Milton Selzer were members of the corrupt, incompetent Town Council. Besides the beautiful Kurt Weill music, the play had a serious point: that democracy, imperfect as it is, is still better than dictatorship. Gerald Savory directed, and Bob Downing was stage manager and advance director for what turned out to be a short summer tour.

Burl Ives was a big man, and hobbling around on one leg in the summer heat in velvet robes could not have been easy. He had a long background as a successful folk singer, but not as an actor. (His Tony Award for playing Big Daddy in *Cat on a Hot Tin Roof* was still years in the future.) At the present time remembering lines was not his strong point, and I distinctly recall his saying to the hero, who he was condemning to death, "You're going to be hanged at sunrise, and . . . and, err — and all that shmegaggy."

Our next stand was at the charming Playhouse in Olney, Maryland, a suburb of Washington, D.C. It is the only theater I have ever seen with a tree growing through its roof. I was told that when the building was enlarged nobody wanted to see the tree destroyed.

Arthur Anderson in *Knickerbocker*.

Burl Ives and *Knickerbocker Holiday* at Mt. Kisco.

The show went very well and everyone was happy, except perhaps for one member of the audience. President Truman was invited as a special guest on opening night, but was early, and so had to sit on one of the wooden benches on the lawn until curtain time. But there was a resident cat at Olney who was also used to sitting there, and when the President arose to go into the theater his tuxedo was covered with white cat fur.

Knickerbocker Holiday then went to Norwich, Connecticut, up the Thames River from New London, and Burl Ives invited Milton Selzer and me to go with him and be the crew on his sailboat, which was moored at the 79th Street yacht basin in Manhattan. We got there late on closing night and slept on the boat, sailing up to Norwich the next morning. As I recall the cast all stayed at a hotel in New London.

During the week's run of the show we went on a cruise on Long Island Sound, and there is no experience quite like being on a sailboat, under full sail on a breezy, sunny day. The only off-putting part of that day's cruise was returning to Norwich up the Thames River, and being met by a submarine, which was based at Groton. A submarine's superstructure is almost as large as a two-story house, and is, especially when it is coming toward you in the opposite direction, as the French would say, "*Formidable!*"

In December of 1949 another call came as a result of the Theatre Wing showcase. Harry Young was the director at The Albany Playhouse, a stone building on Lodge Street which I was told had once been a mill. Most of the actors lived in a brownstone house at 98 Columbia Street, on a steep hill just steps from the theater. There was a communal kitchen, and each of us could do our own cooking, and keep our own food, with labels. It certainly saved a lot of money over what would otherwise have been restaurant meals. That was only a problem when some actors left the company as their engagements were over, leaving food in the refrigerator which eventually went bad and turned strange colors.

Two Blind Mice opened on January 11. It is about bureaucratic stupidity in Washington, and concerns a newspaperman who single-handedly reactivates a long-dormant government agency called The Office of Seeds and Standards in an elaborate plan to win back his divorced wife. I played a well-meaning but feckless young Government functionary. None of the Albany actors were well known, but as with many stock companies, audiences came to see the play, not the stars, and eventually chose their own favorite actors. The basic company included Ed Hunt, Barbara Barton (his wife), Mary Farrell (the director's wife) Judson Pratt, Patricia Ferris and Howard Erskine.

The Playhouse was run by Malcolm Atterbury, a middle-aged, long-jawed, good-natured man. The whole enterprise was possible because he had inherited Pennsylvania Railroad money from his family, and he and his wife Ellen occasionally acted in the shows. He knew, however, that the theater had to pay its own way, and was very careful about money. He once called a meeting of all the actors, and apologized for having to raise our room rent by one dollar to sixteen dollars a week, due to the rising cost of fuel. The cast, ranging from character people to romantic leads, were all good, and well cast by Harry. My pay was $70 a week, five dollars more than Equity scale, and not great even in 1950, but I was getting invaluable experience playing on stage, and enjoying both that and being with the others in the company.

When I first arrived at the theater for rehearsals, a pleasant voice at the box-office window said, "Yes? Can I help you?" It was

Eleanor Harvey, a native of nearby Troy, slim, brown-haired and blue-eyed, who it turned out was also a whiz at all things financial and managerial. We liked each other, and dated and danced and went on drives in her Chevrolet. Dixie Lee, the theater's publicity chief, was certain that there would soon be an Albany Playhouse wedding.

Each Albany play rehearsed two weeks and played two weeks, so there was not the desperate "let's get it on in a hurry" routine of weekly stock which I'd experienced that summer at Keene, NH. While playing *Two Blind Mice*, I was rehearsing *The Village Green*, another pleasant comedy, but not a knee-slapper. After that was finished I returned home, then was called back to Albany in March to play Brinckerhoff in Sidney Howard's *Yellow Jack*.

I had been thinking a lot about Eleanor in the meantime. There was time for that during the three-hour train rides to and from Albany. As much as I was fond of her and wanted to get married, I was much too unsure of myself to make that commitment. When leaving after *Village Green*, I had promised her I would say what was my decision about proposing.

When I returned to Albany she met me at the station, taking an intermission from a cocktail party that afternoon to which we were both invited. She obviously had been thinking, too, about US, and expected an answer from me. As she parked the car, she said, "I'm just drunk enough to ask you." The answer, of course, was no, and I am sure it was devastating for both of us. She was one of the nicest people I had ever known, and I hated hurting her.

Howard Breslin, whom I met doing *Lawyer Tucker*, was not only a successful radio writer but also a novelist, mostly historical. The first novel of his I read was *The Tamarack Tree*, about a Whig convention which took place for three days in July 1840 in the small village of Stratton Mountain, Vermont, and which featured hard cider, ox-pulling contests and speeches by the great Daniel Webster. Interwoven with the historical facts was the plot involving the people who lived there. It was a good adventure story. Howie came from a New York Irish Catholic family. He was a small man, small partly because being hit by a car in his childhood meant that his back was, he said, partly held together by silver braces. Howie and his wife Patricia owned a little wooden house on a hilltop in

Towners, N.Y., which I had never heard of. Towners is nine miles north of Brewster, and one day I put my bike on the train (most trains had baggage cars then) and visited Mountainview Park, altitude 936 feet, which consisted mostly of summer cottages owned by working people from New York City.

In 1949 I bought one of them. House and a half-acre plot were slightly more than $5,000 and I paid off the mortgage in five years from acting earnings, and from renting the cottage for the three summer months. There were two small bedrooms. The living room had pine-paneled walls, and a stone fireplace. On its north end was a screened-in porch where in nice weather you could sit and eat, or just vegetate and listen to the birds. I could take the train to Towners and walk up the hill. It was called Honeymoon Cottage because people said that was all it was big enough for. I eventually did spend part of my own honeymoon there, but that was many years in the future. Meanwhile, there was profound satisfaction in actually owning a house and a piece of land, complete with huge rocks, trees and weeds. There were always jobs to do, which I did mostly alone, to try to improve the house, which was one of several on the hill which had been built during the 1929 Crash. I learned, by doing, a lot about carpentry and other things to do with maintenance and improvement. And it was all mine.

In 1952 I got a call from Aimee Hepting, a fellow alumnus of Professional Children's School. She was a dancer and choreographer. She was to stage an employees' show, which was done yearly by the Abraham & Straus Department Store in Brooklyn, and she wondered if I would be interested in writing some sketches and lyrics. It sounded fascinating, especially as I was planning a bicycle trip to Europe, and this would help pay for it.

The store had some large empty spaces for rehearsals. Aimee was strict with the singers and dancers, blowing a whistle to get their attention. Several people had ideas for sketches, and some of them segued into musical numbers. One older lady, Sophie Sageman, was in a running gag involving English as a second language. "Please to tell me, where are the peelas?" she said. "Well, we've got all sorts of peelers, Madam. Potato peelers, fruit peelers . . ." "No. no, that's not what I'm talking about." "Well, what kind of peelers do you want?" "Peelers to sleep on!" Blackout.

Another number was *Fooling Around in Ladies' Lingerie*, featuring Brescie Thompson as a dandy in Homburg hat, morning coat and with cane who waltzes through the ladies lingerie department and enjoys the annoyance of the people who work there. I wrote the rhyming narration, and the accompanying music was from that slightly risqué song *She Had to Go and Lose It at the Astor.*

There was one performance at The Brooklyn Academy of Music on a Saturday afternoon. I acted as stage manager, running the show, but had never seen the acts on stage — only in rehearsal, and from the prompt side could not see them now. All I could do was to give the union crew, on the intercom, cues for "House to half, curtain up," and so on. Frustrating as it was for me, the audience, which was mostly the performers' relatives, enjoyed the show, and I am sure it was a good morale-builder. The whole thing involved much writing, rehearsing, many subway trips from Manhattan and many frustrations, but was, on the whole, satisfying. My fee for writing and directing was five hundred dollars.

Meanwhile, through American Youth Hostels, I had booked a trip to Europe, and, on May 29, my bicycle and I left on a train to Montreal, the point of departure.

10
CHAPTER
BIKING THROUGH EUROPE AND FINDING MY ROOTS

The *TSS Columbia* was an old tub owned by The Greek Line. The crew was Hispanic and the cabin stewards were German. It wasn't much to look at, but it was seaworthy enough to get us across the Atlantic. From Montreal we sailed first down the St. Lawrence River, then out into The Atlantic, and that night there was the most beautiful display of The Northern Lights — the aurora borealis — that I had ever seen. Most of the passengers were my age or younger, and on very modest budgets. It was easy to get to know people, and again a good respite from my actor's life.

The food was okay, and the stewards before every serving said *bitteschon,* and afterward *dankeschon.* There was a little three-piece band which played for dancing after dinner, and it was a unique experience to dance while the floor was gently rocking. The sea air and the company were good, and an extra pleasure was that everything at the bar was fifteen cents (this is not a misprint). But at those prices you did not have a private cabin, and the young man with whom I shared mine, who was Swiss, was pleasant enough, and spoke good English.

It took the *TSS Columbia* ten days to cross the Atlantic, and then we pulled into Southampton. I cannot say we "docked" because to save money on dockage fees The Greek Line had a little tender pick us up from the ship, and I could see my bicycle being lowered down onto it. The navvy who helped us said he knew all about The Greek Line. It seemed they had a steamer even older than the *Columbia.* It was the *TSS Canberra.* I had seen it on a postcard. The ship was so old that the superstructure above the steel hull was made of wood. The man was most impressed by the *Canberra's* menu. "Djer know wot they 'ad on that 'ere Canberra?" he said. "They 'ad spinach pie fer sweet!"

This was basically a youth hostel trip, and the hostel in London was in a six-flight walkup (how the bicycles were taken care of I do not remember). Another time in London I stayed at a bed and breakfast owned by a professional singer and his wife. My room was on an upper floor, and when I came back from a night out the halls and stairways were pitch-black. I felt my way up the stairway as best I could, and halfway up was startled by bumping into another body — a man sitting on the stairs. He'd had a couple of drinks, he said, and was resting. The blackness I later found was because hallway light switches were on timers, which turned the lights out after a certain number of seconds, to save on electric current. Another energy-saving device was the Geezer. When you wanted hot water you would turn the tap, and the Geezer's small gas burner would heat whatever amount you wanted as it came out.

London, of course, with its historic old buildings and irregularly-shaped streets, was exciting. Another fascinating part was the Underground. When compared to our subways it was much older but in many ways more modern and efficient. Some of the stations are so deep underground that they are reached by elevators, which are unattended. As you pushed a button the door would open, and then a recorded voice would say, in falsetto and sounding like an old 78 rpm record running too fast, *Stand clear o' the gates . . .* At one station the mechanism was slightly defective, and the dignified British voice slowed down at the end of the message, and saying, *Please stand cleah . . . off the gvstzdss . . .*

My first trip out of London was to visit an old friend of my mother's. Traveling by a combination of train and bicycle was so easy because you simply removed your bike from the baggage car at your destination and pedaled off. The lady and her daughter lived a short distance from the station in a u-shaped house which had a luxuriant garden in the center of the u, with sunflowers over six feet high. Next morning I asked my hostess how she achieved this. She explained that they would simply pump the contents of the cesspool into buckets to water the plants. "I know it's not very nice," she said, "but we do have a lovely garden."

I biked around England in a clockwise direction, going as far south as Penzance near the Island's southern tip, then north again on its west coast. Everywhere was beauty and lushness. In British youth hostels you did not prepare your own meals. They were served by the hostel. The food was always fresh and delicious, made better by the fact that you had just cycled thirty or forty miles.

Using the British Ordnance map and the youth hostel guide I could determine where I wanted to go each day. When I could see I was approaching a large manufacturing city, I simply put the bike on a train again, bypassing it. I went as far north as the Lakes Region. One hostel there was not accessible by road. You pushed your bike up a steep gravel path to reach it. And in that northern latitude when you went to bed it was still full daylight.

The only real trouble I had in England was persistent hay fever. Finally, my eyes were so irritated that I could hardly see, and my nasal passages itching, so I went to a doctor, who gave me some drops which relieved the symptoms somewhat. Even though I was not a British subject my visit was covered by the National Health Plan. What it cost me was a shilling — fourteen cents.

Back in London I visited my Aunt Cornelia Brookfield, who lived in a flat with her companion Ellen Hart. Cornelia was tall and rangy, friendly and glad to see me, but had a natural reserve. She and Ellen had both been translators for the BBC during the war. Ellen had written a biography of Alexandre Dunant, who founded The International Red Cross in 1864, titled *Man Born To Live*. Ellen was shorter, and more open. Also living in London was my uncle Edward Brookfield. He had had an honorable career as a naval officer, and now retired was working at a society which did genealogical research. We had a pleasant lunch at a pub, and it was an adventure to get to know another of my British forbears.

In late July I took a Channel steamer to France and a train to Paris, and this time the youth hostel was at Cite Universitaire, a modern campus which was a short ride on the Metro from the city's center. Only two memories of Paris remain. One was inhaling the diesel fumes of trucks and busses as I biked through the city's streets. The other was being in the Eiffel Tower. The elevator takes you silently up, up through the open structure. From the top there are marvelous views of the city and its surroundings. But a much more persistent recollection of the Tower for me was, as the elevator went silently down, seeing a black cat who was for some reason rearing three black kittens on the steel girders, hundreds of feet above the streets of Paris. I have long since wondered whether any of them survived.

Another train ride south took me to the city of Lyons. From there I bicycled down along the Rhone River as far as Cannes on the Riviera, and it was a comparatively easy ride as the road was all either level or downhill. One late afternoon I had my supper at a little outdoor café by the river, and with it drank a whole bottle of *chateau neuf du pape*, having ridden over a hundred miles that day. Other memories of France are pleasant but not very specific. I do recall that on two occasions I couldn't find any lodging, so slept on the ground on my waterproof poncho. The weather was warm, so no harm done. I left France for Switzerland on a series of little trains, which finally landed me in Geneva. The other thing I remember most clearly about my European adventure is that once I had crossed the English Channel to France the hay fever disappeared. Not a trace of that allergy, and what a relief . . .

While in England I was able to get more information about the Brookfield family. My great grandmother, Jane Octavia, was the youngest daughter of Sir Charles Elton, baronet, who lived in a grand stone house called Clevedon Court in Somerset, by the sea in western England. I visited there during my bike tour. It was the only house I had seen, or expect to see, with its own private chapel. In 1841 she married the Rev. Henry W. Brookfield, who was "noted for his keen wit and dramatic power in reading and recitation." It was he who gave the family its name. In generations gone by, members of the nobility were granted coats of arms, which knights carried into battle and displayed at official functions. The Brookfield coat of arms has a diagonal bar intersecting a wheat field, and the rather forbidding biblical motto: *Beware the Reaper.*

Rev. Brookfield and his wife longed for the social atmosphere of London, and moved there in the year of their marriage. It was there that my grandfather Arthur Montagu Brookfield was born in 1853, and in 1857 his brother Charles H. E. (for Henry Elton), the actor. Arthur Montagu, my grandfather, took up an entirely different life. Graduated from Rugby, he embarked on a military career, which was distinguished, but too long to go into here. I will mention, though, that he served with the 13th Hussars, first in India and then in South Africa. From 1885 to 1903 he was a member of Parliament representing principally the hop growers of Rye.

The two boys grew up amid a lively circle of art, politics, literature and science. Good friends and frequent guests at their Chelsea house included authors William Thackeray, Alfred Lord Tennyson and Henry James. Their mother Lady Jane had not only wit but great charm, and was known for her gracious manner and soft voice. A story goes that she had been obliged to lecture her man-servant on one occasion, but that her dulcet tones had so much more effect on him than sharp ones would have had that he burst into tears, saying, "Don't speak to me like that, ma'am. I would rather have a good scolding any day."

My great uncle was sent to Cambridge University, where he won the Winchester Reading Prize. He then studied for the law, but "was never called to the Bar," possibly a polite way of saying that he never actually found employment as a solicitor. In any case he wrote that "I felt I ought to try and earn an income sooner than I had any prospect of doing at the Bar," and it seems to me probable that he had grown to hate it. My uncle had seen a great deal of theater not only in London but in Paris, and was fascinated by it. When he announced that he was *going on the stage*, both his mother and his elder brother implored him not to. But Charles was gregarious and well liked, and was able to persuade managers to hire him. By age 22 he was already with the Haymarket Company, and this began a long series of engagements which never ceased, both in London and in the provinces, as out-of-town engagements were called.

Charles was at the same time a prolific writer. He co-authored and produced between 40 and 50 plays. The most fascinating to me was *Under the Clock*, which appeared on British variety bills (what we called vaudeville) in 1893. It was the first time that Sherlock Holmes had ever been portrayed on stage. Charles Brookfield played Holmes and Seymour Hicks played Watson, and the one-act playlet lasted for 68 performances.

My Uncle Charlie had also acquired a reputation as a wit, and was always welcomed at his clubs — more than one. He said that during rehearsals of a musical comedy, which he probably co-authored, he came upon one of the composers, looking upset. When asked what

Charles H. E. Brookfield.

the matter was, he told Charles that he had heard one of the stagehands strumming one of his numbers on the rehearsal piano — the impudence of the fellow! "Good gracious!" exclaimed Brookfield in sympathetic tones. "And what did you do? Shift some of his scenery?"

A prominent Harley Street physician was roused from sleep at three o'clock one morning by one of his wealthy patients and asked to come at once. Arriving at the house he was ushered into a gay supper party. One of the guests (I can't prove it but suspect it was my great-uncle) greeted him with: "Oh, Doctor! I am so glad you could come. We wanted you to settle a bet as to exactly where the diaphragm is." Furiously angry, the doctor told them not only that but a good many other things as well.

Late in his career, Charles Brookfield was appointed Joint Examiner of Plays, which meant that he and his co-examiner had absolute authority to authorize or refuse the production of any play on the West End. This was met with a lot of criticism, especially because Uncle Charlie had co-authored a play called *Dear Old Charlie* which itself had run into trouble with the British censors.

Before Charles became ill with tuberculosis, which claimed his life in 1913, he and his wife Jane Grogan, who was also a professional writer, had penned a two-volume story of the life, and especially friendships, of his dear mother, called *Mrs. Brookfield and Her Circle*.

After his mother's death Charles retired from acting, and would hardly ever even go to see a play. To complete this turnabout he embraced the Roman Catholic faith, and his son Peter became a priest. In his own chatty autobiography, titled *Random Reminiscences*, he includes this disclaimer: "For personal and other reasons I have omitted nine-tenths of what I remember."

The next Brookfield theater generation included my uncle Eugene, who wrote songs and painted charming little watercolors of geraniums, thatched roofs and winding roads. During the First World War he was a member of the British Artists Corps, whose talents the government sensibly utilized for morale-boosting shows, not to mention the painting of camouflage nets. Eugene had none of the high spirits, or the social contacts, that his uncle did, and unhappily was ignored by the Brookfield family because he was gay. But he was the second generation of a theatrical lineage, and so on my trip I discovered that I in my own career am the third.

At the end of August, having seen my aunt and uncle again in London, I re-boarded the *TSS Columbia*, and on it were many of the young people with whom I'd sailed to Europe. The little clicker on my bicycle showed that I had ridden 1,112 miles that summer.

11
CHAPTER
EIGHT YEARS A BACHELOR

My career after the European trip will have to be put on hold a bit. First I have an obligation to the reader. What good is an autobiography without any mention of my private life? That I had the normal urges goes without saying, but for a long time I didn't do anything about them. Why? Fear? Lack of self-confidence? Or just lack of information? It isn't that I didn't have opportunities. I remember a WAC when I was in the Army Air Force, stationed at Greenville, Texas, who would have been glad to check in with me at the Adolphus Hotel in Dallas, as many GIs did on weekends. Then there was my bunkmate in the barracks who said he knew two girls who would be willing to double-date. Well, I said to myself — why not? We took a taxi from Dallas out to their house. They opened the front door and stood there, side by side — and I was at once turned off by both of them. They were not only ugly, but their front teeth were seriously decayed, and the whole image was a depressing one. I left immediately without making any excuses. I could see the lights of downtown Dallas in the distance and headed that way, but it was a long walk. For sometime after my bunkmate would deride me by sarcastically calling me "Fearless Fosdick," a cartoon detective in the Dick Tracy comic strip.

A providential opportunity came years after my discharge, from an old friend. The Andersons had known Tina and her first husband ever since my childhood on Edinboro Road. She had ambitions to be an opera singer, but several things prevented that. First, her husband left her. Years later she had a second marriage to a man whose ethnic culture apparently included wife-beating, so she left him before long. But during all those years the Andersons and Tina, being old friends, kept in touch. Her marriage to Stanley Jones, a good-looking man with a fine baritone voice, was most happy. But in the late '50s he died of bone cancer, and Tina was alone in her East Side apartment.

I think she instinctively knew that I had never experienced intimacy, and was determined to remedy that, which both of us did one night. I was a quick study, and it was the best introduction to sex I could have had. From then on I began to meet more girls with whom I shared companionship and satisfaction. One unexpected encounter I remember was with a young, rather sad apprentice girl whom I knew from having worked at the Westchester Playhouse. She showed up at my bachelor apartment one Saturday, and the reason was obvious. I didn't find her irresistibly attractive, but who was I to be unkind?

Another girl was Louise (not her real name), who long after our affair was over and I had married Alice showed up at our apartment with her son, a beautiful little boy of about five. It seemed that she had met a musician in Sweden, who unexpectedly fathered the child, and married him. I recall her saying that that foam stuff was no damn good.

I was never promiscuous — it was always one affair at a time, and none of them ended with severe emotional distress suffered by either the girls or me. Also, no one got pregnant. What I would have done about that I honestly do not know.

In March 1953 I got a call from Bob Downing. He and I had remained friends after *Knickerbocker Holiday*, and several times had lunch together. He had written a play, *Around We Go*, about the development and travails of an American family. I was to play Orin, the father. I am afraid that after fifty-five years I don't remember much else about the play, except that it was well-written, and poignant. It was to be done in Houston at The Playhouse on Main Street, which was run by Joanna Albus.

The theater was a circular one-story building. Unlike other arena stages it had walls behind the audience, so that actors could not see the stage until they made their entrances from an outside hallway. There was a red cue light at the head of each aisle. The light would come on for your warning, and when it went out you would open the door and make your entrance. All of us got used to this system, but I never liked it or thought it was reliable.

With no transportation I never did get to see any of downtown Houston. The theater and the excellent Weldon Cafeteria were almost next to each other, across the street from my rooming house. My room was on the ground floor, with no telephone, and there was no carpet on the floor. I didn't mind, as I had become used to all sorts of housing when playing out of town. The weather in March was warm, and I remember one afternoon while at rehearsal leaving an open bottle of Dr. Pepper on the floor. When I came back I was fascinated to see an endless column of tiny red ants, which paraded single file across the floor from the front door, and up the sides of the bottle.

The play was given loving direction by Joanna Albus, and careful rewrites by the author. We had three weeks of rehearsals and four weeks of playing, with good audiences and good reviews, but *Around We Go* was fated not to be seen anywhere after Houston.

After the play closed I went by Pullman for a brief stop in New Orleans, then to Savannah, Georgia, where my mother's old friend Nellie Abrahams, who had given me my first introduction to a professional acting career, was still living. Before returning home I made a stop in Charleston, West Virginia, for a reunion with my old Army buddy George Spruce and his wife Ruth Ellen.

In 1955 I began what was a new cycle in my life and my career. What seemed to be a negative was that in October 1954 *Let's Pretend* did its last broadcast, after a record 25 years on the air, longer than any dramatic program, except *One Man's Family*. Cream of Wheat had cancelled out on December 6, 1952, after sponsoring us for nine years, and the show had reverted to being a sustainer, which meant we were paid not by the ad agency but by CBS, and the fee, which had been $71.25, was now $43. Under the sustaining code two actors were allowed to double without extra pay, and I was usually one of them, as I now did animal sounds as well as acting roles. Nila Mack had died on January 20, 1953; Jean Hight became director, and Johanna Johnson the writer. The magical stories of *Let's Pretend*, and the parts I'd played, ranging from old men to wicked giants to talking horses, and the people I'd worked with, had given me joy and security, and some lasting friendships, but the ending of my long-term subsidy was really for the best.

The positive part of the new cycle began when I read a one-sentence squib in *Variety* which said that David E. Durston had been appointed radio and television director at the Lynn Baker advertising agency. Dave and I had served together in the Air Force at Spokane, WA, and I was in one of the shows he put on there. When I called, he told me that Lynn Baker was developing a new radio show, *Mr. Jolly's Hotel for Pets*. Mr. Jolly, played by Sam Gray, had a home for unwanted animals, and the animals talked to each other, unknown to humans but audible to the radio audience. "Can you do a talking cat?" Dave asked. Of course, I said yes. "Then how about a parrot?" The cat was named Gregory and the parrot was Mr. Farley. The show was drolly humorous, and was meant to appeal to grownups as well as children. It was sold to Puss N' Boots Cat Food, owned by the Quaker Oats Company. Our first show was recorded in April, 1954, six months before the last *Let's Pretend*. *Hotel for Pets* was later done live on the NBC network, starring Frank McHugh, and lasted until March 1956.

In December 1954 I was cast as The Newspaperman in George Bernard Shaw's *The Doctor's Dilemma* for the Phoenix Theatre, T. Edward Hambleton and Norris Houghton, producers. It was directed by my former schoolmate at Professional Children's School, Sidney Lumet. It had an all-star cast, headed by Roddy McDowall, Geraldine Fitzgerald and Sheppard Strudwick. We had a pleasant six-week engagement. The Phoenix, at 12th Street and 2nd Avenue, is now a multiplex film house, but in one of the black-painted screening areas on the ground floor you can still make out the outlines of the original handsome proscenium arch.

The play is about an artist (Roddy) who is dying of an incurable disease, and some of the most prominent doctors in London are sent to cure him, partly for the sake of his lovely and appealing wife (Geraldine), but they are stymied by the fact that Dubedat is a rotter, and completely selfish.

One of the doctors was Will Kuluva, with whom I'd played in *Knickerbocker Holiday*. The doctors all hate The Newspaperman, who is a cheap journalist, bringing in his camera to photograph a dying man. It was Will who opened the door to let me in, and it didn't help my actor's concentration when at every performance he said sotto voce in his guttural Massachusetts accent, "Ged the fug in theah."

The Doctor's Dilemma and other jobs at the time found me, if not well off, enjoying a pretty good, steady income. And that is why one morning at the breakfast table I found myself looking at Apartments for Rent in *The Village Voice*. The apartment I found was still in the West Village, at 289 West 12th Street.

It was in the basement of a four-story brick house, and it was one room and a bathroom. I called it My Sunken Living Room. To save space I bought a lowboy refrigerator, a gas stove which sat on top of it and a little cabinet and counter alongside. The rent was $45 a month. It was no more than adequate by any stretch, but it was all mine, and I had my privacy, and my independence. I still saw my parents about once a week, and had Sunday dinner with them at a restaurant. But all this I know was a shock to my mother. She had continued to be emotionally dependent on me as her youngest child, and now little Tokey was gone.

For the rest of my professional life commercials, voice-over and on screen, continued to be a major part of my income, added to by some joyful experiences in the theatre. The first commercial on camera was for Pal Razor Blades. I was reclining on a sandy beach, which was in a studio on East 4th Street. Another was a live voice-over for *The Campbell Soundstage*, a dramatic show done in the formerly beautiful NBC studio 8-H. I was a friendly-voiced narrator telling how Campbell's had decided to add noodles to their chicken soup: "Oodles and oodles of beautiful noodles!" I said. Well, there was no one I could identify as director. After I'd been at the microphone several hours waiting to rehearse, a young man from BBD&O came over and said, "Read it for me." What he had to contribute, I don't remember. An hour later another fellow from the ad agency came and said, "Read it for me, would you?" And just before we went on the air a third agency man had me do it for him. On the broadcast I did it the way I knew it should be done. And I swear that after it was over all three of them came to me separately and said, "Great! You did it just the way I wanted."

Commercials also paid for my green Lambretta motor scooter. I distinctly remember when I started thinking of getting one. It was while pushing the bike up a hill on the French Riviera on a hot summer day in 1952. Ahead I could see a little spring bubbling up. "Ahh! Just what I need!" I said. But getting closer to the spring I was able to read a sign near it which said, EAU NON POTABLE. And at that moment a little motor scooter came buzzing past me up the hill and that was the start of my motor scooter idea. It didn't turn to reality until after I had moved, and gone on one last bike trip. I got off the train in Portland, ME, and biked up the coast to Wiscasset, then inland to Berlin, NH, where the acrid smell of a paper mill provided one more vivid memory. I went up Mount Washington on the cog railway, probably one of the few times the little one-car steam train had carried a bicycle. There is a weather observatory at the mountain's top, and a sign saying that they had once clocked there a wind of 231 miles an hour. And even in August it was quite cool. I bicycled back down, brakes on all the way, to a little town at the base of the mountain. When I got there, it was growing quite late. I asked, but there was no place to eat, and no place to stay. One of the residents said, "You can sleep in the jail." The jail was dark, unoccupied and unlocked, and the wooden bench I slept on was hard. But next morning, opposite the jail was the old puffer-belly Boston & Maine locomotive ready to pull my train to Boston.

In 1955 I had an interesting variety of theatre jobs, the first at the Pocono Playhouse in Mountainhome, PA. It was quite a trek on the motor scooter, but worth it. We did three plays from Noel Coward's *Tonight At 8:30: Brief Encounter, Red Peppers* and *Hands Across The Sea*, the star being Jane Pickens, with whom I had had that first film job. From singing on radio as one of The Pickens Sisters she had turned to dramatic roles, and aside from her British accent being tinged with a Southern drawl she was quite good. My roles were forgettable but pleasant. Much more satisfying was playing Howard Bevans in William Inge's *Picnic* the following week. Janice Rule was Madge and Louis Edmonds was Hal, and my Rosemary was Mary Jackson. John O'Shaughnessy was the sensitive and helpful director.

Viola Roche was one of my fellow cast members. She and her mother Philippa Bevans were British actresses who both did quite well on the American stage and it was Philippa who supplied what has always been one of my favorite putdowns. In 1961 she was playing the role of Mrs. Pearce, Henry Higgins' housekeeper, in *My Fair Lady*. A visitor backstage one night was her friend Alfred Drake, who had

As Howard Bevans in *Picnic*.

recently opened in *Kean*, a musical version of that famous actor's life. He had gotten enthusiastic notices, but the show was a flop, and had quickly closed. "Why, Philippa," he said condescendingly, "I didn't expect to see you playing such a small part." Her reply was, "Well dear, I'd rather be a shit in a hit than a hit in a shit."

Immediately after *Picnic* was a summer package tour of *You Can't Take It with You* starring Charles Coburn. I played Ed Carmichael. Everybody loved Mr. Coburn as Grandpa Vanderhof, and the six-week tour of summer theaters ranged from Bristol, PA, to New England Mutual Hall in Boston. Meanwhile, I was continuing to do *Hotel for Pets*, occasional dog barks for commercials, and had begun what over a period of years was a series of roles on CBS Television in *Mama*, starring Mady Christians and directed by Don Richardson, who never turned up at rehearsal without his bow tie and red pocket square.

The agent France Hidden, whose office was on West 42nd Street, looked and dressed like a New England schoolmarm, but had a lively sense of humor and limitless knowledge of theatre. In 1956 Francey sent me to audition for *Music Go Round*, a musical stock company in Somers Point, New Jersey, which is 20 miles south of Atlantic City. I became a member of the company, and took off on the motor scooter in June. The theater was a rambling white stucco building that I was told once had been a big night spot in the 1920s; stars, including Rudy Vallee, had played and sung there. There was a long hall upstairs, lined with doors leading to small windowless rooms which would not have been comfortable to sleep in but had obviously been used for other purposes. I am sure it was what British cockneys used to call "a knockin' shop."

The season opened with *Plain and Fancy*. Then we did *Naughty Marietta* (I was Silas Slick), *Kismet*, *Hazel Flagg* and *On the Town*. I was Ozzie, one of the sailors (*I Get Carried Away*). Those roles also call for more than a bit of dancing, and the cartwheel I did was the flattest one you ever saw. Then there was *Show Boat*, *The Wizard of Oz* (I was The Tin Woodman) and *South Pacific*, which was held over an additional week. The routine was not easy, but the summer was a great learning experience. I was expected to know my material before I went down to Somers Point. If I had a solo I would get one individual rehearsal (brief) with Rudy Bennett the conductor. The theater being in the round meant that there was next to no scenery, pretty bare I thought, but a great money saver for Barnard Sackett, the producer.

Business at Theatre Go Round was spotty at best, and on one occasion Charley Mantia from Actors' Equity came down from New York and paid the cast out of the bond that had been posted with the union. To get money to start the next week's rehearsal, the producer took out a mortgage on his father's house. Meanwhile, not fifty feet from the theater's entrance was The Tony Mart, a bar with live music which always did big business.

It was in 1957 that I went to Detroit to play Capt. McLean in *Teahouse of the August Moon* at the Northland Playhouse. After a week there we went to the musical tent at Clio, Michigan. One night after the performance we were given a party at the home of a local lady whose husband as it happened was out of town. As the party was winding down, one of the young actors silently handed me the keys to his car and I drove the others home.

One of my more interesting jobs was that October when I went to the Southampton Long Island Auto Museum to do an institutional film for DuPont auto paints. It was called *The Finish with a Future*. I didn't have any lines, but during the three days' filming was seen driving half a dozen antique cars, beginning with a Stanley Steamer and a Model T Ford. No, I cannot claim that my acting career has been dull or routine.

One more role on what *Variety* called The Citronella Circuit presented itself that summer, when I played The Preacher and The Manual Training Corporal in *No Time for Sergeants*, at The Lakes Region Playhouse and the Kennebunkport Playhouse in New Hampshire. For this junket I also rode the motor scooter there and back — again quite a trip. At Kennebunkport Robert Currier, the producer, needed the sound effect of a car approaching and stopping, so they tape recorded an actual car doing just that. It was, of course, almost inaudible, so I put the effect on tape vocally, and it sounded just fine.

In the spring of 1957 I was at the Coconut Grove Playhouse, Miami, Florida, to again play Howard Bevans in *Picnic*. This time Hal was Rip Torn and Madge was Sandra Church. The theater, then run by John Lane, was a handsome white stucco building with

Spanish accents, and I was most impressed by the goldfish pool in the lobby . . . Only in Florida . . .

Madge's tomboy sister Millie was played by Daryl Grimes, who I was told was coached by her friend Peggy Feury, an Actors Studio alumna, also in the cast at the Coconut Grove. Daryl seemed to be adding mannerisms to the performance it didn't call for, and which were, I thought, a jarring note in a beautiful play. On one occasion she and Peggy spent the day at the beach, swimming and sunbathing, and got to the theater just in time for half hour. That night I thought that Daryl gave her best performance ever as Millie. She was too tired to do the mannerisms.

That fall a longer and more exciting run was in *Auntie Mame*, starring Constance Bennett, produced by Richard Barr (who remembered me from the Mercury Theatre years earlier), Charles Bowden and Turner Bullock. This was the National Company, destined for Chicago. I was to play three small parts and understudy another, replacing an actor who was leaving. I joined the company in Washington at the end of August, played the beautiful Fisher Theater in Detroit for four weeks, and then on to Chicago. There the cast all took more or less permanent housing, and I found a modern one-room apartment on North Clark Street. I could take the subway downtown to the Erlanger Theater in the Loop and in nice weather I could walk there, except on matinee days when the drawbridge over the Chicago River might be up and make me late for half hour.

Chicago was exciting because of its dynamics — the atmosphere was so different from that of New York. Also, I was working in theatre. I got on very well with everyone else in the cast, except on occasion Miss Bennett. Onstage she gave a crisp, authoritative performance as Mame Dennis, with a good sense of the comedy it called for, but offstage she was also playing the role of the actor-manager. I was more than once told by the stage manager to report to Miss Bennett's dressing room, where she gave me notes such as: "MIS-ter Anderson, I think you should give an upward inflection at the end of that speech. Now let me hear you do it." When I left the company, a local Chicago actor, Tony Mockus, took over my parts. He later told me that he then became low man on the totem pole, and was the one who got those notes in Miss Bennett's dressing room. Meanwhile, I was going on to something better.

At Christmas time Chuck Bowden had showed up at the Erlanger. Peter Ustinov was then playing the lead in Chicago in his own play, *Romanoff and Juliet*. It was closing, and a bus-and-truck company was being organized by Bowden, Barr & Bullock, this one to star Bert Lahr. The entire army of the mythical country where the play takes place consists of just two men, and I knew I would be right for one of them, a much more identifiable role than the three bits I was playing in *Auntie Mame*. Chuck Bowden said okay, and we began rehearsals in a hotel ballroom.

Mr. Lahr, with years of experience as a comic in burlesque, Broadway shows and in films, was a little uncomfortable in the role of The General. The crispness and the wit of Peter Ustinov's dialogue were really not suited to him, but he worked during rehearsals to turn the Peter Ustinov role into a Bert Lahr one. His general insecurity showed up when he would try little pantomime comedy bits, and would ask the rest of us, "Is that anything?"

We left Chicago by train in mid-February for Topeka, Kansas, our first stop. From then on we traveled by bus, and most of our performances were one-nighters. The routine of a bus-and-truck tour is this: You are on the bus each day for no longer than eight hours (Equity rules). You then check in to your hotel, where we were guaranteed a maximum room rate of five dollars (remember, this was 1958). However, you do not unpack, because you'll be back on the bus again early the next morning. There is just time to *maybe* rest a few minutes, then dinner, and report to the theater. After the show, there would usually be a place where we could get a cup of coffee, or a drink (except in dry towns). Meanwhile, the crew had struck the set, and was trucking it to the next night's stand.

The theaters where we played were sometimes real legit houses, sometimes converted movie theaters, and in one town we played on a temporary stage set up in a sports arena. During the day's travel some actors slept, some talked, and some played poker. I was usually interested in the surrounding countryside. There was a lot of griping and groaning about eight hours on a bus, though the bus had a restroom, and we did get coffee breaks, and an hour off for lunch.

Bert Lahr was The General, Walter Flanagan and I were the entire Army.

In the play I was First Soldier and Walter Flanagan, my fellow company member from *Auntie Mame*, was Second Soldier. I had a song, for which I accompanied myself on my guitar. Though the soldiers were more or less straight men, we did have a few funny lines, which got laughs. This disturbed Mr. Lahr, who said to us one night, "Look fellas, these parts are nothin'. Don't try to make somethin' out of them." Another night after I had gotten a laugh he said to me, "Don't do that. If you do that I'm gonna catch flies." The next performance I got a laugh on that same line, and he did his catching imaginary flies routine, which got a bigger one. He could not stand to be upstaged, especially by an actor in a minor part.

Our relationship was a little warmer in Houston, Texas, where we had a five-night stand. He called me early one morning to know if I would come with him to Liberty, Texas, where he had an interest in a gas well, and wanted company to go and inspect it. We drove there in his station wagon at a high rate of speed. He had located the gas well, which was an unimpressive arrangement of silver-painted pipes about ten feet high, located among suburban houses. He looked at it and said, "I can't understand it. I'm supposed to be getting royalties from this thing, and nothin's happening."

In March it became obvious to the producers that the B & T *Romanoff* tour had about played itself out, and we closed in Syracuse after eight weeks. The bus let us all out on a rainy morning at 9th Avenue and 55th Street, and Willie the driver took our bags out for the last time. Then I hefted my large metal suitcase into a taxi and returned to my Sunken Living Room.

Bert Lahr was basically a clown, and a brilliant one. Though The Cowardly Lion is the role all of us still remember him for, he got almost as much national notoriety, at least at the time, for his commercials for Lay's Potato Chips ("Betcha can't eat just one"). Besides dozens of appearances in films, in burlesque, television and even on radio, his most enduring accomplishment was his 18 Broadway shows, with two Tony Awards. The *Romanoff* tour was just a minor blip, and it could not have been his happiest experience. Like other stars I have played with, the tremendous ego necessary to sustain his career did not always endear him to other actors, but when I thought of it later I could not help but admire his talent, and his devotion to his craft.

Bert Lahr's last job proved to be the death of him. In 1967, filming extensive night scenes outdoors in *The Night They Raided Minsky's*, he was stricken with pneumonia. His last words before dying were, "Mildred, why aren't my clothes laid out? I've got a seven o'clock call."

One of my more interesting television jobs in those eight years had me on-mike but off-camera, in 1954, filling in for a puppeteer who had a week's vacation coming to him. It was *The Rootie Kazootie Show*, on ABC Television five nights a week at 5:30. What a TV puppeteer does, as most people know, is to work below the stage, hands over his head, simultaneously manipulating the puppet, speaking the dialogue, and watching the action on a monitor. I grew used to it in those five days but probably wasn't brilliant, this being entirely new to me. One frustration of that week was waiting each day for the end of the House Un-American Affairs Committee hearings, prominently featuring Senator Joseph McCarthy, before we could go on the air.

The New York ABC Television studios were, and still are, on West 67th Street, in what had been The New York Riding Academy. There was a huge indoor arena where the horses were trained and exhibited, concrete ramps so they could go from floor to floor, and a balcony where members could watch. With those large and unencumbered spaces it was ideal for television. Another large New York space eagerly grabbed for TV was what had been the Sheffield Farms milk bottling plant on West 56th Street — high ceilings — no vertical columns. Probably no one remembers that now, but for years the CBS studio complex was referred to as The Milk Plant.

Another good stint at the microphone was in the spring of 1954. I was called for a recording of *20,000 Leagues Under The Sea*, at the RCA studios on East 24th Street. It was adapted from a Walt Disney film which came from the original Jules Verne story. It ran for 20 minutes on four sides of 45rpm RCA Victor Little Nipper records. The story was about young Ned Land (William Redfield — we still called him Billy then) who accompanies Professor Arronax (Ian Martin) and his nephew Conseil to search for a mysterious sea monster in the tropical ocean. Conseil was played by Sarah Fussell, who was very good at doing child voices, but since Conseil was a boy her billing became *Sandy* Fussell. Bernard Lenrow, whom I knew from radio, was Captain Nemo, commander of *The Nautilus*, a submarine vessel, and I was the voice of Snoopy the Seal, who saved them all from danger several times. As with all children's stories on records in those days there had to be a signal for the child to turn the record over, and this was Snoopy barking three times, and blowing his horn, all of them done vocally by me.

Satisfying as it was doing commercials on radio and TV, and doing television shows, there was nothing like being on a stage. In 1958 there were two jobs in swift succession, and both of them were emergencies, filling in for other actors in mid-rehearsal. That summer I was called to the Bucks County Playhouse in New Hope, Pa., and was met at the Trenton station by the producer, Wally Perner. It was a Thursday, the fourth day of rehearsals for Jean Anouilh's *Tiger at the Gates* starring Hurd Hatfield. The actor playing Demekos, a poet and leader of the Senate, had been let go, because he either could not learn the lines or just proved unsuitable. I never asked which, or what his name was; just plunged in.

The Bucks County Playhouse was a white-painted building on the west bank of the Delaware River, and New Hope was then as it is now a big tourist attraction. The Playhouse had, originally under the direction of Mike Ellis, gained a reputation as one of the top summer stock houses in the East. We played for two weeks to good houses. Two other cast members I remember were Frances Reid, long married to the late Philip Bourneuf, Sam Kressen, who made a good impression every summer as Benjamin Franklin in Philadelphia during Fourth of July celebrations, and Renie (pronounced Reeny) Riano, who played Hecuba, Hector's mother. She I still recall because she had several dogs, and slept with them in her station wagon because she knew that none of the local inns or private homes would accept that many animals. We closed on June 13, and that date is important to me because five days later I was in Warwick, Rhode Island, subbing for another actor who had to be replaced.

I had received a call from Jack Lenny, an agent who'd known me for some time but had never put me in anything until then. The Warwick Musical Theater, a large tent theater, was doing *The Caine Mutiny Court Martial* starring William Bendix. Jack picked me up in his convertible and drove me up to Warwick. On the way he explained that a friend of his had asked him to do something for this older actor who needed work, and who seemed right for the role of Dr. Lundeen, a psychiatrist testifying at the trial of Captain Queeg. The only problem was, he seemed unable to retain his lines. Jack was disgusted. "I'll never do anyone a favor again," he said.

My housing was all set. Most of the actors were living in an old three-story hotel in downtown Warwick. Warwick had, since the 18th Century, been a textile manufacturing town, but now much of that industry had disappeared, and the only activity I saw seemed to be that of raising mushrooms. The restaurant where I ate, though it was okay, had mushrooms with scrambled eggs for breakfast, mushroomburgers for dinner and mushrooms everywhere.

My hotel room was comfortable enough. The only uncomfortable part was that the old actor who I was replacing had the room next to mine. He had apparently paid in advance, and decided to stay on for the entire week. I felt I had to go over my lines in a low voice, so as not to make him too uncomfortable. The first night I was there he knocked on my door and said, "Would you like me to cue you?" I couldn't bear to do that. To cap the entire situation, the old gentleman had with him his dog, an aging fox terrier which had a heart condition. This meant he had to carry the dog down two flights to be walked, then back up again. The dog's name was Lucky.

We then had another good week, this one at the Oakdale Musical Theater in Wallingford, Connecticut, and I was enjoying doing Dr. Lundeen. However, that memory has been for all these years dominated by the grubby old manufacturing town, the mushrooms, and by the old gentleman and his dog.

Starting with the postwar years I had dated many girls, but was becoming more aware that missing from my life was a close relationship. I certainly wanted to get married, but that seemed to be something in the far, indefinite future. I was discouraged by the women I met, most of whom were, of course, actresses. Some were sweet and some cynical, but all, I thought, driven by egos that I did not feel I could compete with. Nor did I see myself in any long-term live-in arrangement. And so meeting Alice Middleton, to whom I have now been married 46 years, came about through a series of seemingly ordinary events which led us to each other.

Auditioning for TV commercials was for me almost a daily occurrence. I was often sent by Mort Schwartz, a busy, aggressive agent who had gotten me several jobs. One day he sent me to an audition at Norman, Craig & Kummel ad agency at 488 Madison Avenue, which was to be quite a different experience.

Most ad agency casting directors were women, all of them pleasant and efficient, but I was never attracted to any of them. Alice Middleton, however, was different. She had warmth, she had humor, and a very good grasp of not only advertising but theater as well, which I found out during a very pleasant conversation after my audition.

It was several weeks later when our paths crossed again. Ever since the days of *Auntie Mame* in 1957 Dick Barr had continued to call me for his off-Broadway productions. He was a pioneer at bringing new playwrights onto the scene, the most important, of course, being Edward Albee. In 1961 he hired me to stand by for

Gerald Hiken, who played double roles in Jack Richardson's two-part play *Gallows Humor*. In the first part I was Walter, the mild-mannered executioner who has a confrontational scene with his wife (Alice Drummond) as he prepares to go and do his day's work. In the second part I was Philip, the condemned man, who is visited in his cell by a prostitute, also played by Alice, as a paternal gesture by the State, and by the Warden (Vincent Gardenia). The fourth member of the cast was Wyman Pendleton, who delivered a prologue before each part.

In February 1962 Dick Barr and Clinton Wilder presented this play and others with the overall title of *Theatre of the Absurd*, at the Cherry Lane Theater on Commerce Street. I took over the double role in *Gallows Humor*. Then I played Daddy in Albee's *American Dream*, with Jane Hoffman and Sudie Bond. The repertory also included *The Sandbox* by Albee, *Endgame* by Samuel Beckett, *The Killer* by Eugene Ionesco and Albee's *Zoo Story*, in which I played Peter, and Ben Piazza was Jerry. It was interesting and challenging doing different roles in three different plays.

One Saturday night after a *Gallows Humor* performance I encountered Alice Middleton and her friend Patricia Milic backstage, talking with their friend, Wyman Pendleton. Alice turned to me and said, "Hello, Arthur. I'm Alice Middleton. I was very impressed with your performance."

Of course, I said to myself — Alice Middleton *THE CASTING DIRECTOR. ALWAYS BE NICE TO THEM.* This was my actor's reflex. But it was instantly replaced by another. This was Alice Middleton *THE GIRL.* In a mohair jacket and skirt, and a little hat with a snippet of lace below the front brim — so different from the office. Alice was brunette — brown-eyed and slim, and altogether attractive.

I can't recall my exact thoughts during the next week. All I do remember is that between the acts one night I looked up her number in the Manhattan phone directory, called Alice on the pay phone backstage and asked her for a date. I was a subscriber to the Phoenix Theatre, and the play they were doing on East 74th Street was Arthur Kopit's *Oh Dad, Poor Dad, Mama's Hung You In the Closet and I'm Feeling So Sad* — a strange play and a not-too-auspicious choice for a first date, but it did lead to a second date, and many more.

About a year or so before, having outgrown my Sunken Living Room, I was now living on Broome Street, on the Lower East Side, in a lovely apartment with a view of the East River. However, it was many blocks from the nearest subway station, and most of the neighborhood spoke either Yiddish or Spanish. I was lonely there, and decided to move back to Greenwich Village. The apartment I found was on West 13th Street. How much did Alice have to do with that decision? Probably more than I realized at the time. Soon after, she became my girlfriend, and I began finding out who she was.

Alice had grown up in Linden, New Jersey. She first thought of being an actress at age five, and in her teens took part in school plays and public-speaking contests, and after graduating from high school enrolled in The American Academy of Dramatic Arts. Within a year she was also starting to make the rounds at theatrical offices, and was beginning to find extra work in films. After V-J Day she joined a Shubert musical repertory company playing *Rose Marie, Countess Maritza* and *Merry Widow*, and so was now a member of Chorus Equity. That and a summer of musical stock in Atlantic City were beginning to give her a solid theatrical background. In 1946 the USO was sending a company overseas to the Pacific, doing an old 1926 comedy, *Your Uncle Dudley*. Alice was hired as understudy and assistant stage manager.

Her adventures playing for GI audiences in Japan, Korea and the Philippines could fill a book by themselves. The tour lasted seven months. Then, while traveling back to the East Coast by train in May 1947, she made the decision to change her name to Alice Middleton. Her Hungarian name of Miklosy had been mangled too many times, and she was tired of being referred to as "that little girl from New Jersey" by casting people.

A few months later she moved to New York, and lived at The Rehearsal Club, which was in two brownstones on West 53rd Street, a place where young actresses could live inexpensively while making theatrical rounds. In 1949, after gaining more experience in touring shows and summer stock, she was more and more convinced that she belonged on the production side of the footlights, and determinedly set out to get involved in the growing medium of live television. In early 1950 she went to work for NBC network TV as a Production Assistant on dramatic shows.

However, all this started to melt away in 1955 when television began to be taped or filmed, and programs could easily be done from Hollywood with major stars. When I met her, she had been at Norman, Craig & Kummel for several years. Such was the background of the woman I had picked to be my wife, and the wonder of it was that she had picked me.

One of our joys was the cottage at Towners in Putnam County. Alice had never seen either the cottage or the motor scooter, so it was quite a shock to her when she got off the train one day in April and found me and the scooter waiting for her at the little single-track Towners station. I had found a garage in Brewster to keep the scooter, so after weekends at the cottage we would ride there and get the five o'clock train back to New York. Our courtship, as it would have been called in older times, was full of adventure. Dating previous girlfriends had been fun, but I had never felt that close to any of them. My whole life had now changed, though I certainly didn't think of that at the time.

That summer we saw each other only spottily, because I was on tour. The play was *Sunday In New York*, a comedy by Norman Krasna. I played a Japanese waiter and two other small roles. Tommy Sands, then married to Nancy Sinatra, was starred. We opened in Falmouth, Mass., on Cape Cod, and played seven other summer theaters in Upstate New York and New Jersey. Alice was able to join me the weekend we played at The Grist Mill Playhouse in Andover, New Jersey. That theater sticks in my memory because it was right next to a railroad freight line. A long train would pass at the same time every night during the performance. The noise was deafening, and there was no point in going on while the train was rumbling through, so the actors would simply stop and freeze. It took about three or four minutes, but it always seemed like an eternity. I later heard the same story from another actor whose theater was next to a railroad.

Alice had hopped a bus to Andover, and since I had the motor scooter with me that was the only way for us to get back to New York. It was a Sunday, and I had to be at the next theater that afternoon for rehearsal, so we started before dawn in fog and darkness, with our bags strapped to the rear of the scooter. That was a bit scary in the dark, on an unfamiliar highway, but perhaps even more so to me was going through the Holland Tunnel on the little green Lambretta, followed closely by a huge truck.

Professional events during the next few months, whatever they were, were overshadowed by what happened next in our relationship. We had grown close and comfortable with each other, but Alice had to make a difficult adjustment. We did not speak of marriage directly, but I had laid out what I hoped for and expected in a marriage. First, two children, a boy and a girl. The boy would, of course, be named after me. My wife would have natural childbirth, would breastfeed the babies, and all this meant that if it was Alice she would become professionally Alice Anderson, and eventually quit her job. All this from mild-mannered, non-aggressive Arthur. Alice, on her part, had not thought of marriage, much less children, even as a possibility. I didn't realize the turmoil that was going on inside her. And so it was a shock when, just before Christmas, 1962, she told me that she didn't want to see me anymore.

I remember going home alone and hitting a bottle of Cutty Sark. Now Cutty Sark is a good whiskey, but not in the quantity I drank. In a semi-sozzled stupor I called up a nearby florist and had a little Christmas tree sent up. It was still Christmas and there had to be a tree. I can remember crying only twice in my adult life, and this was one of them.

During the next months I would sometimes call the ad agency and ask to speak to Alice Middleton. Alice's secretary, Sandy, would stick her head in the door and say portentously, "It's Arthur on the phone." She said, "I don't want to speak to him." This went on until one Sunday night in June. My phone rang, and it was Alice. There was a discussion program on CBS radio. "Call me back after it and tell me what you think," she said.

Alice later told me that she herself had done a lot of thinking, agonizing, and some drinking, as I had, and finally found that, as she put it, I had grown on her. To give in to all those demands must have been a particular wrench, but she was too honest to say yes and then not follow through. That night Alice's friend on Waverly Place, Maggie Jackson, had been out to walk her Irish setter, and was surprised to find the two of us sitting together on the front steps.

In July, once again seeing Alice, I was cast as Foster Wilson, the hotel owner, doubling as Pawnee Bill, in *Annie Get Your Gun* at the Tinkers Pond Playhouse in Syosset L.I. The leads were George Gaynes and Denise Lor. It was fun to do that show. The only negative I remember was the dressing rooms. They were in a long shed that had been a chicken house years before, and the faint odor of chicken droppings still pervaded the whole building. It was not a month later that I was in *West Side Story*. I had the speaking part of Gladhand, the social director who emcees the dance where the Sharks and the Jets are glowering at each other, and tells the crowd what a good time they're having. We played for more than six weeks at four summer tents. The leads were Anna Marie Alberghetti, David Cryer and Allyn Ann McLerie, who played Anita.

An eventful summer, to say the least. By now I think that there was an unspoken understanding between Alice and me that things could not go on as they had. And one hot, humid night in July (there was thunder far off) we took a walk in Washington Square Park. I don't remember the conversation that led up to it, but as we sat on one of the benches, I said to her, "Alice, I don't want to date you anymore. I want to marry you. Will you marry me?"

(Pause.) "I — I'd like to say yes."

"Well, it's not going to happen unless you do."

(Long pause). "Yes."

And the traditional kiss. Then, to put a dramatic button on it, there was another rumble of thunder in the distance.

The six-block walk between West 13th Street and Waverly Place was now a happy stroll, as we made our plans together. First, we had to have a place to live, and found an apartment up two steep flights at 88 Charles Street. Friends and relatives were invited to the wedding and to the reception at the Grosvenor Hotel across the street from the Church of the Ascension.

Two complications came up, however. The first was that I got a job soon after that could have turned the whole thing upside down. It was a nice part on the TV series *Route 66*. This episode was to be shot in Poland Springs, Maine, and it was uncomfortably close to our projected wedding date.

The script was titled "Same Picture, Different Frame," starring Joan Crawford. It concerned an artist who turned out to be a

In *Route 66.*

murderer, played by Patrick O'Neal, and the location was the famous 75-year-old Poland Springs Hotel, an imposing yellow-painted wooden structure on a hill with a view of the Atlantic Ocean. The sheriff investigating the murder was Tom Bosley, and I was his assistant, Deputy Stone. For this I had to be able to ride a horse, and having ridden once before I believed I could handle that.

There was a tavern which was part of the hotel property, where some of the scenes were shot and where the actors ate. One of them, a middle-aged man, hearing that I was about to be married, said, "Don't let them get the upper hand. Once that happens, you're a goner." This was not particularly encouraging news, but I surmised it meant that his own marriage was not a happy one.

Though the scenes in which I was on horseback were done uneventfully, I remember that Miss Crawford seemed a bit insecure. When she was about to mount her steed, I remember her saying nervously, "Is he all right?," which I am sure meant *Am I all right?* The shooting at Poland Springs went well, though I always had the insecurity of "What if we aren't out of here on schedule?" After all, I was to be married the next week, on Saturday, September 21, and we didn't have the license yet. Thank God, I did fly back to New York on time, on the 13th. Alice and I had a talk with Dr. James Kennedy, Rector of the Church of the Ascension, who had become her friend and counselor.

Then something else happened which could have put her in the hospital, but which I am thankful to say, didn't. The previous January, while she and I were broken up, I had done a repeat of my roles in *Sunday In New York* for Robert Ludlum, producer of The Playhouse on the Mall, Paramus, New Jersey, who incidentally later became a very successful novelist. I was then cast as Baptista in their next production, *Kiss Me Kate*, starring Stephen Douglass and Elizabeth Cole. All of this was well and good, but the second complication turned out to be Romeo.

Romeo was a cat — a beautiful grey-and-white coon cat who belonged to Eunice Brandon, a member of the cast, and her husband, the business manager at Paramus. There was a cast party at their West End Avenue apartment, where Eunice explained that Romeo was being driven nearly frantic from being chased by both their dog and their little four-year-old boy, and his only refuge was up on a bookcase. The upshot was, would I be willing to take Romeo? I had no responsibilities at the time and liked cats, so I thought, *Why not? He would be good company.* And so shortly afterwards I took Romeo in a cat carrier to my third-floor walkup on West 13th Street.

I am sure Romeo was grateful for a peaceful home. So the first thing was to get him a meal. I went to a supermarket and bought two cans of cat food — a brand I didn't know but which seemed okay. I opened one of the cans and put the food in a dish before him. The cat sniffed it, looked at me and let out a most expressive meow which even a stupid human could understand. It said, "I can't eat this!"

Before I went out of town to shoot *Route 66*, Alice had consented to cat-sit for me. After her day's work at the ad agency, she would go to the apartment, feed Romeo and play with him affectionately on the bed. Apparently, they had a good relationship. When I came back from Maine Alice was waiting for me in the living room. I took her in my arms and kissed her. Then Romeo came up behind her and sank his teeth into her lower left ankle, emitting a savage growl. "Get him off me!" said Alice. I picked the cat up and put him in the bathroom.

An animal psychologist would probably know better than I what was going through the cat's mind. All I can surmise is that Romeo didn't know who he belonged to, and the conflict was too much. I got Alice to St. Vincent's Hospital, where they should have given her a tetanus shot but didn't. I called Eunice, told her what had happened, and asked if she could not somehow take Romeo back. She had some friends in Connecticut who had a farm, and as far as I know he spent the rest of his days there, in a better home than I could have given him. As for Alice, the wounds healed, though after 46 years the fang marks on her lower left ankle are still visible.

Though being married is a happy event, I admit that the night before, alone in what was to be our bedroom at 88 Charles Street, I did have the feeling of *What have I done?* Up until now I had just let life wash over me, but this was a most intimate commitment to another human being, and as far as I was concerned a permanent one.

The ceremony at Ascension was not elaborate. Alice, at age 37 (and I was 41), had no intention of walking down the aisle in a white wedding gown. As a matter of fact, it was a simple beige wool dress, and she carried a bouquet of green lady-slipper orchids. Repeating the vows after Dr. Kennedy, "I, Arthur . . . take thee, Alice. . . ," my voice was more than a bit shaky, and it was not one of my best performances. After the reception, we took off in a little red rented car for Lake Mohonk Mountain House, a beautiful rambling old Victorian hotel 90 miles north of New York, in the Shawangunk Mountains.

12
CHAPTER
MY LIFE AS A LEPRECHAUN

Alice and I received some lovely wedding presents, but the grandest of all came from an unexpected source — an ad agency — and it lasted for 29 years. By 1963 I had gained some reputation for doing voices — character voices, dialects and occasional dog barks. In August Doris Gravert, casting director at the Dancer-Fitzgerald-Sample ad agency, then located in the Chrysler Building, called me to audition for animated cartoon spots for General Mills. New cereals were constantly being invented, and marketed, especially for children. This one was an oat cereal with colored marshmallow bits in it to be called Lucky Charms. The marshmallow bits included pink hearts, yellow moons and green clovers, with many more to be added later. The idea was to have a leprechaun be the spokesman.

A leprechaun is a mischievous sprite or elf of Irish folklore, and traditionally if you could catch the little fellow by the coattails he had to lead you to his pot of gold, which meant good luck. But this leprechaun was especially lucky because instead of a pot of gold he had Lucky Charms. So why not let his name be Lucky? Logical thinking.

In August I had read for the role of Lucky at Dancer, as we actors called it, and so had many other New York voice-over actors. Then there were callbacks, which meant some people were eliminated and others re-auditioned — part of the routine of ad agency commercial production. I don't remember how many callbacks I had. I do know it was before the Screen Actors Guild contract required that actors be paid after the second callback.

My final audition was for the President of General Mills — a white-haired gentleman with blue eyes and silver-rimmed spectacles, who had flown in from Minneapolis, and had final say. This, after all, was to be a long-term commitment, though I had no idea of that at the time. In fact, for the first recording session in early October, I had merely written in my engagement book:

DFS — VOICE OVER — CEREAL RON COLBY DIR.

The fee, SAG scale, was $70. I expected it to be a pleasant two hours' work, which it was, then on to whatever would be my next job, or audition.

The session was at Fine Sound, a former ballroom at the Great Northern Hotel on West 56th Street. The recording companies were glad to get hotel ballrooms to record in. They were all in midtown Manhattan, near the advertising agencies, and had large unobstructed spaces with no columns. And the hotels I am sure were glad to get long-term leases instead of occasional bookings for social affairs.

The Leprechaun was a good-natured little fellow, each time using a different bit of magic to escape the children who tried to catch his Lucky Charms. He always failed when the magic went wrong, but the story ended with everybody happy — all in 30 seconds. Every spot, whatever the plot, always included Lucky's phrase, "Part of this complete breakfast," with a brief live shot of toast, juice and milk. This was referred to by the agency as "the legal shot," and was included no doubt to satisfy government agencies which were monitoring children's nutrition — at least I hope they were.

Over the years the DFS copywriters created countless situations for Lucky to be involved in, the basic plot being the same in every commercial.

Here was Lucky cheerfully minding his own business when the little boy and girl (they never had names) spied him and said something like: "There's Lucky! Let's get his Lucky Charms!" Then the Leprechaun would instantly create some new bit of magic to escape. Once he took off in a hang glider which crashed, with no injury to Lucky, of course, and once in a red balloon, which the little boy punctured with a blow gun, causing Lucky to fall from the sky into a convenient haystack.

Lucky

There were always catchphrases for kids in the audience, and their mothers, to remember, including "magically delicious" and "marshmallow-y delicious!" A little musical couplet was at the end, with Lucky singing:

FROSTED LUCKY CHARMS, THEY'RE MAGICALLY DELICIOUS!

. . . and even today people who hear I was the original voice of Lucky will sing it to me. Talk about product identification! If the agency and General Mills knew this it would bring joy to their hearts.

Arthur and Friend.

In later years there was more audience participation. Lucky would travel to different countries to escape the kids, and there'd be an announcer (Allen Swift) who would say: "Lucky's traveled to a country shaped like a boot. Can you tell which one it is?" There were many premiums, sometimes in the Lucky Charms boxes, and others for which you would send in two proofs of purchase. Since these varied by regional markets and by time schedules, brief announcements could be added at the end of each spot (in radio they were called hitchikes) in which Lucky would say, for instance, "And in specially marked boxes of Lucky Charms ye'll find a coupon fer which ye can get a real four-leaf clover." My favorite premium (this one cost $6.95) was a 16-inch-high Lucky doll made of felt, with an impish expression. He sits in an honored spot in our living room.

When I realized that this job might last some time, I couldn't help but be amused that on *Let's Pretend*, for 18 years my training ground for doing voices, I had never once done an Irish dialect.

A wonderful perk of my 29 years as Lucky was that Doris Gravert had called me directly, and so there was never any agent's commission to pay. Anyway, when residual payments for the replays of the Lucky spots began to come in, I really didn't see the need to try to get more money.

I was now a member of the pantheon of voice-over actors who were long-term animation film spokesmen (no women) for General Mills cereals (see illustration). The many other actors prominent in cereal voice-overs included Joe Silver. Joe had a particularly strong, resonant voice, and claimed, "I don't use a microphone. I just shout into the tape."

During my career I have worked with many other talented and clever voice-over performers in TV and radio. One of the most successful was Allen Swift. Allen got so much work that he opened his own voice-over studio. That way, in addition to session fees, he would also receive rent for the studio's use. His original background was doing stand-up comedy schtick in Catskills hotels, then doing all the voices on *The Howdy Doody Show* in early live TV. One of Allen's most successful radio voices was that of Papa Strohman for Strohman's Bread. It lasted for 32 years — longer than my leprechaun. He is now retired, and his son Lewis J. Stadlen, and grandson Peter Stadlen are both actors.

A clever voice-over actor (sometimes called a voice actor, a label I dislike) may try several voices at the audition, each separate and unique, and the ad agency director can select the one he likes best. There were and still are some actors whose voices are so distinctive that they are virtual trademarks, and they are never expected to "do a voice." One was the late Mason Adams, who, besides being a successful actor on stage and on TV (*Lou Grant*), was for many years the spokesman for Smucker's jams and preserves. His mantra: *With a name like Smuckers, it has to be good!* He was once auditioned by a young ad agency director, who, not knowing Mason's reputation, asked him to try some other voices. "Look," said Mason. "This is what I do." The implication was, "If you want some other voices, get yourself another boy."

Bunch of characters Ever wonder who the people are who supply the voices for those fanciful cereal commercial characters? Well, here's a rare glimpse of them. At a special recording session for General Mills cereals are (l. to r.) Arthur Anderson, the "Lucky Charm Leprechaun"; Peter Waldren, "Booberry"; Russel Horton, the "Trix Rabbit"; Jim Ducas, "Count Chocula"; Larry Kenny, the "Cocoa Puffs Cuckoo Bird," and Bob McFadden, "Frankenberry." The spot is scheduled to air next week.

The faces behind the voices.

Early in my Leprechaun years I was shown sketches of Lucky, in color. He was a little fellow who wore a dark green hat with a shamrock stuck in its light green band, a light green scarf thrown over his shoulder, and, of course, green shoes, with brass buckles. He had a shock of red hair, blue eyes, and always wore a cheerful smile, except when in trouble. The original animators were Hanna-Barbera, and one of my dearest possessions is an acetate cel they gave me with three drawings of Lucky.

Lucky's voice was in the upper register, and his Irish brogue had a lilt to it. It couldn't be too Irish, though. Deed Meyer, the director for most of my 29 years as Lucky, once said on the talkback: "When you say 'cereal' with that slight Irish trill on the 'r,' people in the Midwest won't understand it." And so forever after, whatever other Irish pronunciations I used, it was always "cee-rrr-eal." He was right, of course. I was there to sell a product, not have fun doing a dialect.

Lucky Charms is not confined to the United States. A friend of mine visited Ireland, where leprechauns come from, and the commercials are played there, too, of course. But an Irishman he talked to didn't quite believe my dialect. "You can tell it's a Yank," he said.

All went swimmingly between me and Lucky, or between me and DFS, for about fifteen years — a long period, indeed. Then I was told that the agency was trying the idea of a different spokesman for Lucky Charms: Waldo the Wizard. Waldo, it seemed, was a bit kooky — lovable but bumbling. He would make mistakes and the kids would pounce on his Lucky Charms. Several animated spots featuring Waldo were made, and shown in test markets. This meant that TV stations in smaller cities would show them, usually in early morning hours before children went to school, or on weekends. People were questioned at shopping malls: What TV shows did you watch yesterday — or today? What about the commercials? Do you remember a wizard? What product was he advertising? Did you/are you going to buy it? And so on in that vein, product identification being the name of the game. The cereal business was and still is highly competitive.

I was then not called for any Leprechaun spots for months. Silence from DFS. Nor did I call them to say what the heck is going on, fellows? Whatever I said was not going to change their minds anyway. It was disturbing, though I should add that I was continuing to get residuals from the Lucky spots which were running nationwide.

Then after many months had gone by, I got a call for a Lucky Charms recording session. It was at 799 7th Avenue in the CBS recording studios. There were friendly hellos all around, and then I went into the recording booth, got down to business and recorded two or three spots, as usual under the strict direction of Deed.

Only after I was finished did I go into the control room and say, "Deed — what's going on? What about the wizard?"

"Arthur," he said. "The wizard is dead."

They had apparently decided in their corporate wisdom that Waldo had not worked out, and let's stay with Lucky. Thank you, God.

A couple of years later Doris Gravert called and said, "Arthur, it's only fair to tell you that they're auditioning other Leprechauns." Another reminder, if I needed one, that acting is essentially a freelance profession. Each Lucky session was an individual call and an individual contract. And even if there had been a long-term contract there would have been no assurance that it would be renewed. But I continued to be called. Saved again.

To create a Lucky Charms spot (abbreviation for "spot announcement"), the basic concept and the writing are done at the ad agency. At some recording sessions I was given a storyboard in addition to the script. This is a small series of drawings showing what is happening in each frame, with sound effects indicated. In our storyboards a magical transformation was usually indicated by "SPLINNNGG!!") Storyboards were useful, but I was always grateful to have a script. It was easier to make changes, cuts or other notes. Once the voice track has been recorded, the basic drawings are sent to an animation studio, and music and sound effects are added. And so a 30-second spot may take months before it is finally ready to go on the air.

The children who catch Lucky were needed at most of the recording sessions, and I got used to fresh new juvenile faces every year or so. Adolescent voice change was affecting the little boys especially, and they no longer sounded childishly cute. It was hard to keep track of them as replacements were made. I remember walking down Fifth Avenue one day when a six-foot-tall young man with a deep voice said, "Hello, Arthur. Remember me? I was the little boy on the Lucky Charms spots." Of course I didn't, but said something polite. This happened more than once.

As we were telling a complete story in 30 seconds, every word and every second counted. There was usually a separate take for each sentence, and the voice-over director would say, "Do it three times," and then pick the one he liked best. It was up to the actor to give a different, individual reading for each of them, sometimes for a single word. For instance, if the word were "Zowie!" that called for some fast thinking and creative acting. How many ways, after all, can you say "Zowie!"? And how fast can you figure that out? I think that is one reason only a very limited number of actors are successful in the voice-over talent pool at one time, especially for animated cartoons.

Diedrich Meyer, who everyone knew as Deed, replaced Ron Colby in about 1964. He was sparely built, with blondish hair and horn-rimmed glasses. He said that he had been working for an ad agency in some other capacity, and happened to be passing a studio control room one day when animated spots were being recorded.

He thought that looked interesting. He was able to snag a job as an animation director, and later became one of the agency's most valuable people. He thought quickly; saw exactly what was needed and how to guide the actors. This was precision work, and he knew enough not to call actors who could not deliver. Time was money.

Deed Meyer lived on West End Avenue, and when the agency was on Madison Avenue he would ride his bicycle to work, until arthritis finally made that impossible. I never knew much else about him. During Deed's sessions there was no time for personal chit-chat, and when the actors were finished he would go right to work with the engineer to do final editing of the soundtrack.

Voice-over actors are expected to work quickly and make instant adjustments. Deed might say, "Arthur, I need you to cut two seconds off that sentence." This requires the actor to have two mindsets simultaneously: First, give that line the proper meaning and emphasis — an actor's task — and at the same time cut those two seconds — you might say a technician's task. At the time I wondered why I was tired when those two-hour sessions were over — tired but exhilarated.

Voice actors usually work singly, not in groups as we did in radio, and in a small booth. Everything inside and out is black. The heavy latch on the door is exactly like a butcher's meat locker. This insures complete soundproofing, and given all this it is obvious that anyone with claustrophobia should stay out of the voice-over business. The actor stands at a microphone, in front of which is a music stand with the script on it, a little spotlight illuminating the script, and earphones to hear the director. The third member of the team is, of course, the engineer, invaluable in this precision operation. At first sound recording was done on discs. Once audio tape was invented, about 1947, it was then done on quarter-inch tape, which the engineer would edit by splicing it with a razor blade.

Tape, of course, is now long gone. My first inkling of this was after one of my last Lucky sessions, in 1992, when I was conversing with Deed in the control room. The engineer said, "Will you please move? You're standing in front of the monitor." The recording and the editing were now all done digitally, on the screen — no moving parts and no razor blades, and it was much easier and faster all around.

Over the years the Lucky Charms Leprechaun became a national icon, rivaling Tony the Tiger and The Jolly Green Giant. Though traditionally critics do not review commercials, I do remember that one writer in an advertising article referred to Lucky as "that hapless leprechaun." The comic strips did not neglect Lucky Charms, though. One cartoon sent to me depicts a busy chemical laboratory with steaming, bubbling retorts and beakers. The head of the lab reports to the owner: "I'm sorry, Dean Wilbur. The boys have tried everything, and though your cereal is delicious, it's not *magically* delicious." In another a man sits at the breakfast table. His bowl is upside down, with cereal and milk in his lap. Meanwhile, his mug has spilled black coffee all over the table. The cereal box next to him reads: "UNlucky Charms."

As in all of merchandising, changes have come not only to cereals but to their boxes. Lucky the Leprechaun now has huge, googly eyes, as do all the General Mills cartoon characters. The charm of the little fellow is gone, and he is now a cartoon of a cartoon — whatever it takes to sell in the very competitive cereal industry.

In early November 1992 I got a call for a Lucky Charms recording session, which two days later was cancelled — not that unusual — but the call was not rescheduled. Two weeks after I received a letter from Deed Meyer that read:

Dear Arthur:

I suspect the contents of this letter will come as no surprise. Advertising, like real life, is full of changes. And now the decision has been made to change the voice of Lucky.

Well, Arthur, you have had a long illustrious run. And on behalf of the entire agency and our client I want to thank you for many years of your splendid performance.

Ironically, I won't be far behind. Before next year is out I plan to retire, so Lucky will have to do without either of us. I suspect he'll survive, but he'll never be quite the same.

I'm very grateful to this business, for it has given

me the opportunity to work with talented people like you. Once again thanks and the best of everything to you.

With pompous regard,
DEED
Deed Meyer
Vice President, Recording Director
Saatchi & Saatchi Advertising

Part of my reply was as follows:

It has been as you said a phenomenal run since my first session in October 1963. That's as long as *Tobacco Road, Chorus Line* and *Life With Father* put together.

I am most grateful to the agency, to General Mills, but most of all to you. You have never let me, or any actor get away with doing less than our best, and for that I thank you, as well as for your very nice letter.

With best wishes always,
ARTHUR

Deed did retire to New Hampshire where he owned property, and where he had once been a partner in a summer theater.

Let me not suggest that I have acquired any inside information on the advertising business. I have learned some things about it from an actor's point of view, but anything else except Lucky's past history — how commercials are now produced, for instance — has certainly changed since 1992. Losing Lucky did not make me feel bitter, or even disappointed. Twenty-nine years, after all, is a damn good run for any actor. And what a wedding present! But I must confess that I have never seen or heard the present-day Lucky. I sleep late on Saturday mornings.

13
CHAPTER
87 PERRY STREET

Alice and I got settled in our two-flight walkup apartment at 88 Charles Street, and she went right back to work at Norman, Craig & Kummel. I, meanwhile, started making phone calls to agents to the effect that I was very much available.

My first job after the honeymoon was in Tampa, Florida. It was a new picture to be called *Black Like Me,* based on a true story by a journalist who had his skin dyed to find out first-hand what it was like to be treated as a negro. He applied for a cashier's job at a small supermarket. I was the manager, and told him that the best I could do was to give him a job in the stockroom. The star was that excellent actor James Whitmore. He died in February 2009, and had once mentioned that this was his favorite film role.

After the one-day shoot I rented a car and visited George Rasely, my singing teacher from eighteen years before at The American Theatre Wing Professional Training Program. George was delighted to see me again, as was his wife Helen. However, a change had taken place. He had had a stroke and could no longer speak. I remembered a little French song he had taught me and sang it for him, while George sat there and smiled his familiar beatific smile.

In November I had an unusual late-night shoot doing a commercial for Keebler's Crackers. It was a pleasure to work with my friends John Seymour, third generation of a distinguished acting family, and his wife Abby Lewis. They were an upscale couple returning from a posh social gathering, and exclaiming how delicious the Keebler's Crackers had been. I was the jolly coachman driving them home in a horse-drawn carriage. Every coachman I have played, or even seen, has always been jolly. This was shot in Beekman Place, a

The newlyweds.

quiet street east of First Avenue in the 50s. It is a short street not directly connected to any noisy avenues, so ideal for a sedate carriage ride. This was my third contact with horses. I had not dealt with a horse since my teens, then coincidentally had ridden that one in *Route 66* just a few weeks before. We did several takes, clip-clopping up Beekman Place with the camera truck leading, then re-shot the scene in close-up without the horse.

Riding with the camera was the assistant director, who gave me and the others orders on his bullhorn. This worked fine except for one thing. It was after one AM and everybody on Beekman Place had gone to bed. A woman appeared in her nightgown at the front door of one of the houses and complained loudly about the noise, and why didn't we let them all get some sleep?

What could have been one of my most successful commercial jobs never got off the ground. This time I was called by the McCann Erickson ad agency to be Herman the Butcher. It was for Westinghouse Refrigerators — *You Can Be Sure If It's Westinghouse.* The pitch was that having one of their refrigerators was *Just like having a meat market in your own kitchen.* Here was Herman the Butcher, with German accent of course, dressed in traditional white apron, straw hat and sleeve garters, working at his butcher block and telling us what a pleasure it was to always give the customers fresh meat. After I had auditioned, re-auditioned and gotten the part, a kind lady executive at McCann Erickson confided, "You better get yourself an agent, Arthur. This is going to be big." We filmed two or more commercials in February which were to be shown in test markets, and they took still photos of me in my butcher shop to be used in full-page color ads in magazines, which would break at the same time as the TV commercials. It was for me a series of pleasant adventures.

Then there was then a period of silence while the ad agency did market research on how consumers would respond to their campaign, which I am sure was to be nationwide. Then one day I received a phone call from them. After what I am sure was the expenditure of quite a bit of money the whole thing had been scrapped. It seemed that children had become so fascinated with the German butcher and his meat market in the refrigerator that there had been several incidents reported of little boys risking death by climbing into their own refrigerators and making believe that they were Herman.

My father had retired from the Mack Truck Company in 1950, and did better working for them as a consulting engineer on assignment than he ever had on salary. Alice and I often saw my parents for Sunday dinner at a Greenwich Village restaurant. It was in May 1964 that we got a phone call at the cottage. My father had suffered a stroke and was in the hospital. We rushed back to New York in our rented car. He died on Sunday night, May 4, 1964, which was merciful. Otherwise, he would have been a helpless invalid. The next day I was filming a commercial for Ice Blue Secret deodorant. I was a ship's purser. The mood on the set was subdued, as everyone knew that I had to be gotten out of there as soon as possible to make arrangements for my father's funeral. He was buried in Oakwood Heights, Staten Island, not far from the stone house on Edinboro Road on the hill, which he had loved since 1917.

George Christian Anderson was a man of gentleness, strength and great ability, but not assertive. Perhaps as a result he was not always appreciated or treated well by my mother, and sometimes even by us boys. It was not until after he was gone that I truly recognized his qualities, and the love he had felt for all of us. He comes to mind every time I see a Mack truck go by.

In June I got the role of Colonel Pickering in a touring summer production of *My Fair Lady*. The director was Bill Francisco and the stars were Allyn Ann McLerie as Eliza Doolitttle, and her husband George Gaynes as Professor Higgins. I had worked with both of them the year before, with George at the Tinkers Pond Playhouse and with Allyn Ann in *West Side Story*. George's background was more as a singer than as an actor, but as the summer went on he became more assured as Higgins, and Allyn Ann, who was stronger as an actress, became more and more secure in singing the role of Eliza. Alfred Doolittle the dustman was excellently played by Robert Sinclair, as was Higgins' mother by Jean Muir. It was quite a good cast. I know that Pickering has many times been cast as an older man, but at age 42 I felt comfortable, enjoyed the nine weeks, and I think gave a creditable performance, and Alice was able to join me some of the weekends. I got several nice reviews in the theaters we played.

On opening night at the Westport Country Playhouse I saw someone completely unexpected. It was Freeman Hammond, for whom I had worked 25 years earlier as a teenager in that magical adventurous season of summer stock at Keene, NH. He had a table on the lawn outside the theater, about to do interviews for the local radio station, WMMM. I now regret that I didn't stop to talk to him and ask what he had been doing since Keene, but in the excitement of the opening night I settled for a brief "hello."

Our summer tour included the Northland Playhouse near Detroit, and following that we traveled by train to Toronto, where we played in the only real theater of the tour — the beautifully restored Royal Alex. Our closing two weeks were at East Hampton, Long Island, at the John Drew Theater. Alice came out to be with

With George Gaynes and Allyn Ann McLerie.

me there, and I was able to see that my mother, now widowed and alone, was put up at the Sea Spray Inn.

Alice and I had planned that after we were married she would continue working at Norman Craig for a year, then quit, and we would go abroad. In September we sailed from Pier 40 in the Village on the *S.S. Niew Amsterdam* of the Holland America Line. Anyone who has traveled by ship knows that it is totally different from flying. There is fresh air, room to move around, and always delicious meals in one of the ship's dining rooms. We visited England, my uncle Edward and my aunt Daisy and her husband Roland Browne. My uncle Eugene took us for a brief stroll along the Thames in Richmond, the London suburb where he lived. There was also a side trip to The Ancient Town of Rye, and Leasom, the grand house where my mother had spent her childhood, then a little bus to the village of Appledore, where my aunt Cornelia and her friend Ellen were waiting for us to join them for tea in their garden.

Then on to Copenhagen to meet my Danish relatives. Werner Jenssen, the son of my father's first cousin, of course, spoke perfect English, and immediately took us to see The Little Mermaid, Copenhagen's favorite tourist attraction, then to his parents' apartment for dinner. Though Einar and Emmy spoke no English and we no Danish we got along famously, and the Danish food was, of course, delicious. The next day we traveled north to Elsinore, Hamlet's castle, where a pair of black swans was swimming in the moat. We sampled more wonderful food and then were off to Amsterdam for a brief look-see. We arrived at commuter time, and the heaviest traffic was in the bicycle lanes. We watched the busy canal boats, then stepped in at a little pub for a cool Dutch beer, and were greeted warmly by the "host," a large black poodle by the named of Achmed. Another unique adventure.

It was quite a long train trip to Paris, but we were anxious to experience a European rail journey. The Eiffel Tower and the lights of nighttime Paris were beautiful, but now it was time to share with Alice something she had always wanted to do — tour the wonderful French Chateau Country. Ten days of fairy-tale chateaux, formal gardens and French history — her dream come true. Our group got a lot of attention from the French lady who was our guide because there were so few of us. It was late September and most of the American tourists had gone home. Because neither Alice nor I had Southern drawls or Midwestern twangs the other Europeans thought we must be Canadian. Before leaving France we were able to take a one-day trip to Nice, where Bert Bertram and his wife Rubee had an apartment on the Cote D'Azure. If you looked sideways out of their living room window you could just see the Mediterranean. We had been friends for years because their late son Arthur, who had died of Hodgkins in his 30s, and I were fellow members of the PCS Alumni Association.

Though many things happened in our marriage and our lives we didn't plan, this one we did: In the autumn of 1964 Alice became pregnant, and I was thankful that I had my income from commercials, because any trips out of town would for some time now be out of the question. But, providentially, in May of 1965, I got a call to play in *The Group*, to be filmed entirely in New York. And again I would be directed by my former PCS classmate, Sidney Lumet. The picture was based on Mary McCarthy's successful novel about eight graduates of a girls' college who remained friends. One of them, Pokey Prothero, was played by Mary-Robin Redd, and I was to play Pokey's husband. The large cast included many experienced New York actors, including Kathleen Widdoes, Hal Holbrook, Leora Dana, Russell Hardie, Philippa Bevans, Robert Emhardt, Polly Rowles and James Broderick. They were joined by attractive actresses new to the screen, among them Joan Hackett and Shirley Knight, but none, of course, was to match the future success of Candice Bergen, who played Lakey, the leader of the group.

The scenes I was in included a wedding at Grace Church, a funeral at St. Mark's In The Bowery, within walking distance of our apartment, and a wedding reception at The St. Regis. I got three weeks' work out of it, and, though Pokey's husband was not a major part, I did have the quiet satisfaction of working in what was a major motion picture.

By the spring it had become obvious that we would need a larger place to live. We considered the Upper West Side of Manhattan — for about ten minutes. Both Alice and I really thought of Greenwich Village as our home, and resolved to stay there. The new apartment we found was at 87 Perry Street, on the corner of Bleecker. It was in an old — I mean *very* old — three-story house, stucco on wood, built in 1815 we were told. There was a store on the ground floor, the Andersons on the second, and our landlady on the third. Perry Street was and is a charming, tree-lined street, while Bleecker Street is rather busy, and on Friday evenings is jammed up as cars converge on their way to the Holland Tunnel. The rent was $185 — not bad in those days, though, of course, you could not rent more than a closet for that price now. It wasn't far from the 7th and 8th Avenue subway lines. Our nineteen years at 87 Perry were happy, and as you will see I very seldom lacked for work. Amy Violet (Violet was my mother's first name) was born Saturday, July 24, at Mount Sinai Hospital. Alice had had some bleeding during the first three months of her pregnancy, but it seemed nothing to worry about. The birth was normal, and a few days later we brought our daughter home.

As I demonstrated from my Lucky Charms years, commercials have been a godsend, not only for me but for many actors with families to support. Alice in her professional life had worn several hats, one of them in the production of live television, and knew many fine actors whom she was able to help stay in the business by encouraging them to do commercials.

Though I never did, some actors doing especially well in commercials or other jobs find it pays to incorporate themselves for tax purposes, and think up exotic names for their companies. One actor called his BUPKIS Productions, and Bob Kaliban's corporate name was my favorite: TTMAR Productions, TTMAR standing for Take the Money and Run

I have been many places and helped sell many products, most of them forgotten, but there are a few which stay in my memory. I was a mailman eating with friends at a Shoney's restaurant in Atlanta. I was a man who preached "feed a cold, starve a fever" for Bayer Aspirin, which we filmed in the large kitchen of a church rectory in Brooklyn. And I was inside the (huge) engine of a car, touting the virtues of Dowgard anti-freeze for your radiator. Then I was a druggist, and my customer was Joe Bova, who came in and said, "Can you help me? I want to apologize to my stomach, for all the pepperoni, and garlic and onions." I helped him apologize to his stomach by giving him Di-Gel. Then I was the installer of a gas water heater, and that was filmed in Houston, Texas. Photographs were also taken for magazines, of me with the gas heater, looking pleased. As often happened after filming commercials, someone would ask the actor to do a shot which was a private joke for the agency. In this one I completed the gas heater installation, then asked the camera, "Say — where do I plug this thing in?"

One of the more exotic locations I worked at was The New York Stock Exchange. The spot was part of the series touting New York State, always accompanied by the singers crooning, *I . . . love New York . . . .* In this one I was the Exchange's night watchman, and as I made my rounds with my watchman's clock I mused on the small New York companies which had become great, ending with, "Makes you feel kinda proud, doesn't it?" We filmed this after midnight when cameras, lights and sound equipment could be placed on the trading floor, and we finished about six AM.

Everyone was pleased with the spot — until the soundtrack was played back. No one had realized that, in spite of all the Exchange's new video monitors and other modern equipment, the beautiful oak floors had never been replaced, and as I walked and did my lines, every step was accompanied by a loud "c-r-e-e-e-a-k." So I was sent to a studio where I lip-synced with myself. The final result came out beautifully.

I have been sent to many other locations outside New York for filming. One was the Casa Loma Castle in Toronto, where I was the inventor of "Awake," a delicious orange drink, and was kidnapped by bad guys who wanted to steal the formula. Just as interesting and closer to home was The Douglas House in Orangeburg N.Y., just across the George Washington Bridge. It is a comfortable white clapboard house which sits on large grounds with a swimming pool, and inside are living room, den, kitchen, and upstairs bedrooms, including a boy's room and a girl's room. All of these rooms can be quickly redecorated in period or modern to suit the filmmakers' needs, and there is heavy-duty wiring, and wild walls. A wild wall is movable, so that cameras can shoot the same scene from either direction. I have shot at least two commercials there, plus a featurette for the Nickelodeon Channel, part of a series *The Pioneers of Television.* In this I was Butch "Laredo" Clydesdale, the inventor of the blank cartridge, which saved the lives of several extras, *even real actors* in TV Westerns which had to be filmed in a hurry.

Almost as much of an adventure of filming on-camera commercials was auditioning for them, in which the actor tries to give the advertisers what they want, with the help of the casting director. When my old *Let's Pretend* friend Sybil Trent, then casting at Young & Rubicam, was auditioning a young actor, he became resentful and said: "Are you — *directing me?*"

"Yes," said Sybil. "I'm trying to help you get this job."

In the late 1940s all ad agencies had a Wollensack audio tape recorder, and the actors would act out the spot at the head of a long conference table. When video recorders came into use it was easier for everyone, as the actors would now be in a studio with only the casting director, and she (it was usually a woman) would select the best takes, which would be played back later for the creative people.

If the agent or casting director tells the actor beforehand what kind of character is wanted, he can at least approximate what that character might be wearing. I know of one case where these lines of communication went disastrously wrong. At Young & Rubicam a group of actors were waiting to audition, for Pepsi-Cola I was told. As they sat on benches in the reception room all had beards, or mops of hair, gold earrings, rolled-up sleeves, and some had tattoos on their arms — a surly bunch. Then in walked another actor wearing a white shirt, neat tie and blue blazer with brass buttons. All of them looked at this misfit, and one of them finally asked him, "What are you here for?"

"The agent told me it's a pilot," the other actor said.

"You fool!" he was told. "It's not a pilot — it's a *pirate!*"

This was topped by the actor Mort Marshall. When he was told this story he said, "Must have been a Chinese agent."

Long before cell phones, most actors subscribed to message services, who would always know where they were in case a call came in. Mine for the longest time was Artists' Service (SUsquehanna 7-5400). Eleanor Powers was always cheerful and efficient, and over the years became a personal friend.

The nighttime operator was Bill Burbage, who I never met — a bit older and with slightly sour manner. When Bill was on and I was told he had a message for me, I would always say, "Did you desire me?" And when I needed an early-morning wake-up call I would say, "Wake me in the morning, mother, for I'm to be Queen of the May," and he would always give a long, slow chuckle.

If the actor got a callback after an audition, then later maybe a second callback this was an especially nervous time, as a national on-camera commercial might mean not only session fees but possibly thousands of dollars and years of residual payments for replays. Unexpectedly, the first person to call you if you had the job was not the agent or the casting director but the wardrobe lady. She had to have your sizes immediately because you might be needed to film the spot the very next day.

Over the years many actors have made extra income by modeling for still pictures. If you made a business of it, and were included in an agent's sheet or book, it might be quite worthwhile. Modeling, however, has never been unionized, and there has always been a wild variation in hourly rates, and particularly the waiting time between job and check. In my early modeling career I was paid $50 an hour — seldom more, though I know that things are better now in that department. High fashion models have always been an exception, of course, and some ladies with exceptional faces/figures do make thousands. Some of my jobs for still camera, though, have been interesting, and sometimes fun. One photographer, Howard Fischer, used to call me for the "true confessions" magazines, which purported to tell actual stories of crime or violence. In one I was the husband of a woman who was in the next room giving birth to a child by another man, and in the headline in the front of the article I was saying *LET IT DIE!!!* In another I was a detective struggling with a girl who was a violent criminal.

Most of my modeling jobs were more cheerful and benign. United Airlines had a special fare deal so your wife or significant other could come along very inexpensively, and there was a picture of me and Barbara Anson waltzing out of town Jackie Gleason-style, with the caption *Take Me Along!* My most involved modeling job I suppose was for Ivory Liquid Soap, to keep your hands beautiful while you were doing the dishes. Their spokesperson was always Mary Mild, in maid's uniform. For this I had my earliest call ever — 3:00 A.M. I had to report to the photographer's studio, which was in a former power substation (very high ceilings) on the Lower East Side. We were driven to a public park in Greenwich, Conn.,

"Take Me Along" for United Air Lines.

the reason for the early hour being that the morning light was best. Here I was sitting on a bench with my wife and holding her (very tender) hand, while Mary Mild hovered over us like a patron saint, holding a bottle of Ivory Liquid. She was suspended from a cherry picker in an invisible harness. We had lunch at a local diner, and were back in New York by two o'clock.

The last modeling job I recall was years later right near home. It was for a medication designed to prevent heart attacks, and to alert readers to the danger they needed several photographs of a man having a heart attack, so that the art director could later select which heart attack was best. I had to stagger around various back streets of Greenwich Village having heart attacks, while the photographer followed me with his hand-held camera. This was an exercise in improvisational acting, but complicated by one thing; a group of little boys had noticed us and were following, improvising their own heart attacks just out of camera range.

When television was live from New York there were always interesting jobs. On *Hallmark Playhouse* I worked with Alfred Lunt and Lynn Fontanne playing one of the three law clerks of Justice Oliver Wendell Holmes in *The Magnificent Yankee*. And for years I was on *The Guiding Light*, which started on radio in 1937, went on television as a fifteen-minute program, then half an hour, then a full hour. First the shows were live, as in all television, then taped. I might be a waiter, a hotel reservations clerk, then a funeral director.

One impressive hour show, *As the World Turns*, done at CBS, involved the elaborate wedding of two of the principal characters, which took place in a castle in Scotland. For this they wanted both a Catholic priest and a Presbyterian minister, and I was the priest. I didn't have that many lines, but the cast, the setting, the flowers and the number of extras were all impressive. I had once read of a Hollywood character actor who decided to live his part for the entire shooting day, and I thought I'd do the same, complete with Irish accent. The result was several inquiries from the make-up and then the technical people to the effect of, "Are you really Irish?," then "Are you really a priest?" I said yes each time. I don't recommend this to every actor in every situation, but I think that on certain occasions living the part can be very helpful. In any case, it was fun.

Half-hour series comedy shows were also being shot in New York, and I had several roles on two of the most successful. *You'll Never Get Rich*, starring Phil Silvers and created by Nat Hiken, was the first one. Silvers was so outstandingly good that it eventually became known as *The Phil Silvers Show*. He played Sergeant Ernie

Bilko, an expert at finagling and manipulating people. The producers saved much money by having three film cameras rolling simultaneously, so that doing a new set-up for each shot was eliminated. The producers could simply choose which parts they wanted from each. This way it was as flexible as live TV, and the picture quality vastly superior to a kinescope. Another show I played in more than once was *Car 54, Where Are You?*, which was shot in an out-of-the-way studio in the Bronx.

In 1963 Jack Lenny called me again, this time for *The Jackie Gleason Show* at CBS. They needed two actors to be in sketches and blackouts. There was no audition. I just showed up at rehearsal. Many of these bits lasted only seconds, while Ray Bloch's orchestra played a delicate soft-shoe theme in the background. In one there was a busy street corner with a little old lady and a little Boy Scout waiting to cross (traffic noise heard). But instead of the Boy Scout leading the little old lady across, the lady picked up the Boy Scout and carried him across. Blackout. Alice was in the audience, and said to the person sitting next to her, "See that little old lady? That's my husband."

The other blackout actor was Phil Bruns, and we often did these bits together. My favorite had Phil in white lab coat, experimenting with a foaming potion in a beaker. He swallowed it, grimaced in terrible pain and collapsed under the lab table. In seconds a hairy monster rose up — that was me — holding the empty beaker and saying, in a takeoff of a popular medication slogan of that time, "And it doesn't upset my stomach!" Blackout.

The producers wanted this to be authentic, and so they went to Bob O'Bradovitch of NBC, who apparently specialized in beard and hair work, to make the monster. I had several sessions in his studio with a breathing tube up my nose while the facial hair was applied over a foam rubber mask. I also had hairy hands, and the resulting monster was suitably repulsive. It got a laugh, of course — but all this for a bit that couldn't have lasted more than 40 seconds, total. As I knew this was an important milestone in my acting career, I brought my camera to the studio on performance day, and had Phil photograph the monster.

But this is not the end of the story. When the picture was developed I had some 8X10 copies made and brought one to Bob

The monster on the Gleason show.

at NBC. He was very grateful. "I was so proud of that monster's head and hands that I displayed them on a cabinet in my studio," he said. "Then somebody stole them."

Every actor is called upon from time to time to do parts which will result in little or no payment, but they are a way of learning so you do them. One of mine was in May 1965. The Institute for Advanced Studies in Theatre Arts, or IASTA as we called it, had since 1958 been recruiting directors from many countries to do experimental productions. *Mary of Nijmeghen*, from an unknown writer of the 16th Century, was a morality play in which an innocent girl was seduced by the devil — a female Faust. The distinguished director was Johan De Meester, from Amsterdam. I do not remember the complicated story of Mary's conversion, but do recall most clearly that I was The Pope. The other thing that I remember was Mr. De Meester's direction one day at rehearsal to the actress who was playing Mary. In one scene in which she was particularly despondent she burst into tears. "No," said Mr. De Meester, "I don't want you to cry. I want you to make *me* cry."

In the summer of 1965, shortly after Amy was born, I was back at the Bucks County Playhouse, playing in *The Solid Gold Cadillac*, the Howard Teichmann-George S. Kaufman comedy which starred Imogene Coca. By then Amy was little more than a month old, but Alice was able to come and see the show, while one of the apprentices baby-sat Amy in my dressing room.

Summer stock called again a year later when I played two weeks at the Moorestown Theater opposite Nancy Walker in Leonard Spigelgass' *Dear Me, The Sky Is Falling*, a Broadway success of 1963. It is about Libby Hirsch, the overbearing Jewish mother whose business is everyone else's. I was Paul Hirsch, her husband. Though it was about a Jewish family, and neither Nancy nor I were Jewish, it didn't matter. Comedy is comedy. Critics and audiences loved what one critic called "her flat voice and duck walk." And another critic wrote, "Anderson as Libby's husband, a Sunday golfer, is at his best drunkenly displaying his 'hole in one' pin to the canasta club."

After our first week I was able to drive back to New York with Nancy, and got to know her a little better. When she and I were in the eighth grade at PCS, she was Nan Barto, daughter of Dewey Barto, half of the vaudeville team of Barto & Mann. He was short enough to always get a laugh when he walked between Mann's legs. Nancy's husband was David Craig, a much-sought-after vocal coach who taught actors (including me, later) to perform at singing auditions.

David and Nancy had a Siamese cat who was a member of the family, but did not approve of their long absences when they were off for weekends. He made it known, she told me, one time when they came back home from a particularly long stay. They had in their Sutton Place apartment a gorgeous Duncan Phyffe sofa with three silk cushions, which the cat was strictly forbidden to ever go near. When they entered their living room that Sunday night, as Nancy described it, the cat said, "In there." Then they discovered that he had methodically shat, once on each of the three silk cushions. *Dear Me, The Sky Is Falling* got good laughs and good houses for the entire two weeks.

On nice weekends when I was not working we had established the habit of renting a car and driving up to the cottage on Mountainview Road. One Saturday in July of 1967 the weather was rather sultry and humid, and we decided to stay home. That Saturday morning the phone rang at 87 Perry Street. It was the agent Peter Cereghetti. "Get right up to the Royale Theater," he said. "They've got a ticket for you to see the matinee of *Cactus Flower*." This was the Pierre Barillet-Jean Pierre Gredy French comedy success which had been translated and directed by Abe Burrows and produced by David Merrick. It was having a healthy New York run, starring Barry Nelson and Lauren Bacall. Mr. Burrows was rehearsing the National company, starring Hugh O'Brian and Elizabeth Allen. They were in the third week of rehearsal, but there was a snag in the production. An actor both Alice and I knew, who had been cast as the lecherous Senor Sanchez, was just not able to learn his lines, and they needed a replacement. *It seems to me I've traveled this road before*, I said to myself. I saw the matinee and walked over to the old Criterion Hotel, where they were rehearsing in a ballroom. I knew I could do the Brazilian accent, and it was a good comedy part. I read for Abe Burrows and, having just been burned, he asked if I thought I could get up in the part in a short time. Luckily, I was able to recall for him a few of my many weeks in summer stock, with one-week rehearsals, and said I knew I could do it. He hired me on the spot. This was a big upset for the Anderson family, but as always Alice supported me. I left with the company July 29 for Central City, Colorado, the opening engagement. But, of course, Alice and Amy would have to stay home.

Central City was originally a silver mining town. It stands on a mountain, 45 miles up the road from Denver, "the mile-high city."

The lecherous Senor Sanchez in *Cactus Flower.*

When the mines began to peter out, Central City became a ghost town. Then in 1932 some Denver society ladies thought that the Central City Opera House, built 54 years before, would be a good place for summer entertainment. The theater was not too long a drive from Denver, and within a couple of years operas were again being done there, as well as plays and concerts. The house was now also being used as a tryout spot for shows which would later tour. The town came to life again, with restaurants and other businesses, and when *Cactus Flower* arrived it had long been quite a busy tourist attraction.

And what about housing for the actors? Opposite the theater and a few steps up the hill were pleasant bungalows, painted green and kept in very good shape. These it turned out had been the living quarters of the town prostitutes the miners patronized. Since we'd be there for five weeks I felt able to bring my family, and after *Cactus Flower* opened I rented a car and went to meet them at the Denver airport. I hadn't told them I would be wearing a mustache, goatee and a cowboy-style straw hat.

Amy was just two years old, and I was able to arrange a crib for her. I would sleep late on performance days (seven days a week) and Alice and Amy would be waiting across the street in the Myrna Loy Park, then we would have breakfast together. Obviously, Miss Loy had played there, and donated the little plaza.

Claude Powe, editor of the weekly paper *The Tommy Knawker*, became a friend, and one of his friends took us on a sightseeing tour of the region. This included traveling into the adjoining town of Leadville down the steep hill known as The Oh-My-God Road.

The air in Central City is clear and refreshing, and in the summer there was a brief shower every afternoon, right on schedule. Audiences were friendly, and it was an altogether pleasant stay. On September 2 we all went to Denver Airport. My girls went home to New York and the company on to Washington, D.C. And there we had to make adjustments; a larger set, but more important, more critical audiences, which Abe Burrows knew we'd find in D.C., Detroit and then Chicago. So we did some re-rehearsing prior to the Washington opening, and he had some important things to say to the cast.

ABE BURROWS-ISMS

Good acting is listening. The great actors are the great partners. Help the other actor get his moments. You come off better.

Today [first day on the new set] is the first day you meet the furniture. Don't complain about the furniture. If you were a Greek actor you'd be working with stones.

A laugh is like a horseshoe. Learn to ride it — speak just past the crest — not let it die. [If you do] the boat has sailed.

Central City was like a party. [The audience] were so grateful to see somebody live on stage. Anyone who mentions Central City gets slapped in the mouth.

In Washington Alice was able to see me in the play for the first time, while her parents were baby-sitting Amy in New York. And here it is worth noting that Hugh O'Brian hosted the cast after the show one night at a party in a skyscraper nightclub overlooking the city. He had already treated us to a day at a dude ranch in Colorado. Hugh had been a frequent guest of President Johnson at the White House, and was also able to arrange for us to meet Vice-President Hubert Humphrey, who was very nice to us. Notices were good at the National. Then on to Detroit, where I'd been briefly with *Auntie Mame* ten years before.

My first night in Chicago was in a depressingly sleazy hotel. The next day I found 40 East Oak, an apartment hotel very near North Michigan Avenue and the Chicago landmark Water Tower. Our twelfth-floor apartment would overlook Lake Michigan, and I knew it would be a delightful place to bring Alice and Amy.

Cactus Flower opened in September at the Blackstone Theater, a short subway or bus ride from 40 East Oak and within steps of The Loop. And on September 23 I was able to bring the family to The Windy City.

Abe Burrows protected his investment in *Cactus Flower* first by directing it, also by hiring his son James Burrows as Production Stage Manager. Jim went on to become one of the top film and sitcom directors in Hollywood, and *Cheers* was only the first of his many successes.

Cactus Flower has a rather flimsy plot, which involves Stephanie, a starchy dentist's nurse, Elizabeth Allen, secretly in love with her boss, Dr. Julian Winston, played by Hugh O'Brian. Julian, meanwhile, longs to end his affair with Toni, Ethelynne Dunfee. He tries to get out of it by saying he can't possibly marry her because he has a wife and three children, and asks the nurse to play the part of the non-existent wife. The play was an impossible farce, but it is carried forward more by the cleverness of the dialog and the acting style than by logic. Abe Burrows directed us to play it full tilt, the way in which it was written.

Though we had settled in happily at 40 East Oak, I had a responsibility back in New York — Lucky the Leprechaun. I was able to continue with Lucky by flying to New York on Sundays, recording the latest spots, and then getting back to Chicago on Monday in time for half hour. I was also able to visit my mother, who was by now living at The Association Home, a senior residence on Amsterdam Avenue and 103rd Street, which was so old it had been started for widows of soldiers who had fought in the War of 1812.

Hugh O'Brian was born in 1923 in Rochester, N.Y. He was an athlete in his teen years, enlisted in the Marines at age 17 and became their youngest drill instructor ever. After his discharge he started acting in a Santa Barbara, California, stock company, then was discovered by the director Ida Lupino. What one blurb describes as *His lean, rugged pyhysique and exceptionally photogenic mug* helped his extensive movie career, but none of his films gained Hugh as much fame as his six-year run starring in *The Life and Legend of Wyatt Earp*, which began on TV in 1955. He had long before made an important decision — to change his name. He told me he knew that he would never be a success with a name like Hugh Krampe.

Shrewd investment decisions have made Hugh O'Brian a wealthy man, but from what he told me he is proudest of having founded HOBY, The Hugh O'Brian Youth Foundation, which for many years has trained young men and women for positions of leadership.

Elizabeth Allen came from a solid background of films and Broadway musicals. Though it at first annoyed her, for years she was best known as the girl who had introduced the Jackie Gleason TV show by saying, *And a-w-a-a-ay we go!* She was described as *a tall, willowy brunette*, as tall as Hugh O'Brian, and they made a good team in *Cactus Flower*. Liz as a teenager had been noticed by a photographer as she walked down Madison Avenue, which led to a five-year career as a fashion model. She played Juliet in the original New York cast of *Romanoff and Juliet*, which led to five Hollywood roles and a Tony Awards nomination for her as the female lead in *Do I Hear a Waltz?* So I think snagging her for the role of Stephanie was as fortunate for Abe Burrows as was getting Hugh O'Brian as Julian.

40 East Oak was good for all of us. Robert Howell, Rector of St. Chrysostom's Church, had lent us a TV set, which was how Amy was introduced to *Mister Rogers' Neighborhood*. We had visits from relatives who were in or near Chicago, as well as from Chubby Sherman from The Mercury, who was in town with another show at the time. Another good thing was that two sisters lived on a floor above, and whenever there was an after-the-show cast party one of them would baby-sit so that Alice could be there.

Our Chicago stay in *Cactus Flower* was the scene of a complete change in our family's life. We had already noticed that Amy, though healthy, had not walked at a normal age, or started to talk. Nor did she react normally with those around her. Dr. Shafton, recommended by a Chicago agent who had taken me around on casting calls, examined her. He turned out the light and shone a flashlight on the wall of his examining room, saying, "See? She doesn't follow the beam as I wave the light around." Amy was examined at a Chicago hospital and her case was analyzed by Dr. Vuckovitch, an eminent pediatric neurologist. His verdict was a devastating one: "Global immaturity of the central nervous system." He added that he thought it would not be wise for us to have more children.

We quickly decided that I would leave the show and we would go back to New York and start to deal with our daughter's problem, which we did in May of 1968. Work would be waiting back home, I knew; besides Lucky the Leprechaun, many new things did indeed turn up. But except for that downbeat finish, my ten months with *Cactus Flower* had been good ones.

14
CHAPTER
BACK FROM CHICAGO

In May the three of us walked up the stairs at 87 Perry Street and I turned the key to our by-now-slightly-dingy apartment. While I had only a dim idea what opportunities our post-Chicago life might hold, both of us knew that it would bring new problems we had never dreamed of. The first thing, of course, was to notify casting people that I was back in New York, and work did resume in TV voice-overs, radio spots and on-camera commercials. As much as I loved being on stage that would never have afforded a living, especially for a family that was now three.

Thanks to my agent Peter Cereghetti another role on stage did present itself soon after: *A Mother's Kisses*. This was a musical based on the book by Bruce Jay Friedman. It was about a possessive mother and her young son, whom she sends off to camp. I was the camp doctor, with coke-bottle glasses and a foreign accent, and doubled in another role. The star was Bea Arthur, and Bernadette Peters was the love interest. It was directed by Bea's husband, Gene Saks, with whom I had worked at Mount Kisco, and choreographed by Onna White. We rehearsed in New York and opened at the Shubert Theater in New Haven, then on to the new, modern Mechanic Theater in Baltimore, where we closed two weeks later, a total run of only three weeks.

Alice had seen the show in New Haven, and didn't want to be discouraging, but it was obvious to her that the humor of the Friedman book did not translate to the stage. I think the actors, as actors do, had convinced themselves that this was going to be brilliant, and all of us worked with enthusiasm.

My next part was a small but interesting one in the film *Midnight Cowboy*, directed by John Schlesinger. I was the hotel manager who ejects Jon Voigt when he tries a scam involving one of the female guests. We shot it at the Gotham Hotel at 54th Street and 5th Avenue, late at night so the hotel's business would not be interrupted. In my first shot I was at the front desk arguing with Mr. Voigt. In the second shot I am actually throwing him down the front steps. A stunt man was ready to do this so that no one would get hurt, but Mr. Voigt insisted on doing it himself. The result was that when I pushed him down the steps I went down too, and ended up face down on the sidewalk with a bloody nose. I was taken to Lenox Hill Hospital, and that was the end of my work on *Midnight Cowboy*.

In 1972 the casting director Jessica Levy called about a role in a film to be called *Night Walk*. There is a young man reported missing in action in the Vietnam War who unexpectedly knocks on his parents' door one night. Though they are not aware, but the audience is, he is a zombie — the living dead — and only survives by killing people and drinking their blood. I really didn't want to be involved in a horror film, and told her so. She called again in two weeks, and I said yes. If someone wanted me that much, who was I to say no?

Night Walk was being filmed in the small town of Brooksville, Florida, and the motel where I was put up was right next to Weekeewachee Springs, a tourist attraction which featured underwater swimming mermaids. The young man was Josh Mostel, son of Zero, and I was Ben, the Postman. There was a scene where the family was having lunch on the lawn, and I was invited to join them. After their son left, I said, "I think he oughta see Doc Blanchard. He looks a little peaked to me."

During the several days while we were filming outside the white house on a pleasant, tree-shaded street a middle-aged man struck up a conversation. He was a local resident who told me that he had once been kidnapped by Martians who landed in a flying saucer. I told him this was an interesting story, and since I was Roger Frammis, a reporter for IBC, the Irrational Broadcasting Company, I would like to interview him, and so the next day I brought my tape recorder. The tape, which I play occasionally, is one of my cherished souvenirs. His business card reads:

"JOHN F. REEVES — FLYING SAUCER CONTACTEE"

The film, bankrolled by a Canadian firm, if not called *Night Walk* may now possibly be known by the title *Death Dream* and be available from some obscure website. Great it wasn't. But scary it was.

Due to Peter Cereghetti I had auditions for several Broadway musicals. You would bring your music and accompanists would follow very well, as long as you did not expect them to transpose to another key. If it was really important you would bring your own coach, who, of course, had to be paid. Mine was Fred Silver, with whom I also studied, and we had worked on possible audition songs together. But none of this had resulted in any job.

The musical play *1776* is based on how the Continental Congress, after much bickering, finally signed the Declaration of Independence in 1776. To those who have never seen it the subject may sound dry, but the play is humorous, musically lovely, and often exciting. The show, which had been running since March 1969 now needed two male understudies, since Equity actors were entitled to a vacation after a year in the cast. There were auditions, and callbacks, and auditions, and callbacks ad infinitum. I don't know how many times I stood on that stage and sang, *Siddown, John, Siddown, John . . . For God's sake, John, Siddown — Someone ought to open up a window . . .* , but to my recollection, it was seven. Finally, on a gloomy day in January 1970, I was able to call Alice and tell her that, thanks to Peter, I had a contract.

Though I had acted in many shows in many places, my past experience on Broadway was limited to the Mercury Theatre 32 years before, that depressing one-night run in *The Good Neighbor*, and being Assistant Stage Manager in *Little Dark Horse*. And now, finally — back on Broadway! . . . to me, a significant event in my career. And so as I got to the stage door of the 46th Street Theater for my first rehearsal with Peter Stern, the stage manager, my heart was pounding a little. I came to the door and . . . it was locked! The stage doorman was out on his lunch break. I could only laugh. That'll teach you to overdramatize yourself.

I understudied a total of seven roles in *1776*: The Reverend Jonathan Witherspoon of New Jersey, Lewis Morris and Robert Livingston of New York, Josiah Bartlett of New Hampshire, James Wilson of Pennsylvania, Charles Hewes of North Carolina, Roger

Sherman of Connecticut, and I once played Andrew McNair, the custodian, for Bill Duell so that he could do a lucrative commercial. My fellow understudy was Evan Thompson, married to Joan Shepard with whom I'd played on *Let's Pretend* during our nine Cream of Wheat years. As a result of this Alice and I, and Amy too, were invited to celebrate New Year's Eve with the Thompson family for several years.

The classic question of non-theater people has always been, *How do you remember all them lines?* My less-than-classic answer, at least for *1776*, is that I covered so many parts that when I came down from the dressing room each night I was playing I really didn't remember a thing — but when I took my seat on the stage for the character I was to play, it all clicked into place. None of the roles I played were the leads: Adams, Hancock, Rutledge and so on, but as the script was written each of the smaller roles was also essential to the balance of the play and the audience's understanding of it, and so none of the roles I played were boring or frustrating. As understudy I might get a week's notice to go on in each part, or ten minutes — just time to get into costume and wig. When not playing, there was always solitaire in the dressing room, and when I did play there was an addition to my salary.

Any actor who has understudied on Broadway will tell you that Saturday morning rehearsals can be confusing, especially if you're covering several parts, as I was. You may speak a line as one character, then answer yourself from the other side of the stage as another. Then the following Saturday you may rehearse as someone else.

From Perry Street each night I'd take the Number 10 Eighth Avenue bus up from Abingdon Square and on the same bus was usually Jack Gilford, then playing at another Broadway theater. During the day there were often commercial auditions and sometimes film shoots. It was all in all a happy time.

In late January 1970 an invitation came from President Nixon for the company to perform at The White House on Sunday night, February 22, to mark Washington's Birthday. Stuart Ostrow, our producer, realized that this was a great honor, and good publicity for the show, but he called a cast meeting to say that unless we voted unanimously to do it the date was off. The vote was indeed unanimous. Cast members and spouses were invited, and we all flew down to Washington that Sunday morning.

There was only one other snag. The White House had asked that the song *Mama, Look Sharp* be cut. We were then in the midst of the Vietnam War, and the song's lyrics tell of a Yankee soldier who asks his mother to find him on the village green as he is dying. It is a powerful, poignant anti-war message. However, the management, led by producer Stuart Ostrow, told the White House that unless the song was included we wouldn't be there that night. I am happy to say that he won his point.

The performance was in the White House's East Room. A stage had been built for us, which, unfortunately, meant the actors' heads were only about three feet from the hanging crystal chandeliers, but it did not matter. The audience, which included many senators of both parties and other dignitaries, thoroughly enjoyed it. It was the first full-scale, full-length Broadway musical ever presented at the White House. Music was by the Marine Corps band, led by our own conductor, Peter Howard. Evan Thompson and I were, of course, there that night, but didn't get to play. No cast member wanted to miss this.

There was a reception after the performance, and all of us got to meet the President. The only postmortem worth mentioning is that the next morning Howard Da Silva, our Benjamin Franklin, was out in front of the White House, picketing to protest the Vietnam War.

If there is anything predictable about show business it is that it's unpredictable. After I'd been with *1776* for a year something that looked better presented itself. In March 1971 George Abbott was to direct a revival of the Ben Hecht-Charles MacArthur play *Twentieth Century* in Florida, presumably to then bring it to Broadway. It starred Eli Wallach and Anne Jackson. I got the part (not an understudy) of Grover Lockwood, a business man traveling on the train with his mistress, and gave notice at *1776*. Then on to Florida.

The first notable event there was that when I went to pick up my luggage at the Ft. Lauderdale airport it had been either lost or stolen — but let that pass, as Elizabethans used to say. We opened February 21 at the beautiful Parker Playhouse, the only theater I'd ever played in which had no Saturday night performance, as the audience was mostly geriatric. I was quartered at a lovely motel, complete with palm trees, swimming pool and birds singing. I had promised Alice that I would phone the morning after our opening, and when I did she told me that the night before Amy had had a seizure and been taken to St. Vincent's Hospital. There was no question of immediately rushing home. I was under contract, and as it turned out Amy and Alice had spent only the night there, and were now back home, with our daughter presumably okay.

Grover Lockwood wasn't an important enough part for Mr. Abbott to spend much time on it. But there were chances for me to observe his ways of working, and his quick insights. I also heard two additions to the George Abbott legend. The best known, of course, is the young actor's question to him during rehearsal: "But, Mr. Abbott, what is my motivation for crossing to the fireplace?" His quick reply: "Your paycheck on Saturday." There was also the young assistant who during rehearsal break in a Philadelphia tryout was invited by Mr. Abbott to join him for dinner. He at once had visions of a delicious repast at Bookbinder's. Instead, they walked down an alley to a little diner with a row of stools at the counter. "I'm going to have a bowl of soup," said Mr. Abbott. "What are you going to have?"

Our only other stand as it turned out was The Coconut Grove Playhouse, where we opened two weeks later. The play, which Mr. Abbott had originally directed in 1932, was about a slightly hysterical producer (Wallach) with a production planned, but no script and no money. He is on the train to try to persuade his former mistress (Jackson) to sign a contract, which will guarantee he will get backing for the new play because she has just won an important acting award. The Pullman car actually moves, revealing different compartments for each scene, and also revealing a strange assortment of other characters, including two stranded actors from a German passion play and an escapee from a mental institution. With 20 principals and that moving set, it was a very expensive production. However, with all that work and all that money, it just didn't come together. Headline for one review was *TWENTIETH CENTURY GOES OFF THE TRACK*. The play was lively and witty, and some critics thought it had some great moments, plus that moving train, but that it was a little dated. For one thing, there were three acts, and the pace never picked up. Drastic cuts were made, turning it into a two-act play, but that wasn't enough.

Now that the tension was off Eli Wallach threw us a closing night party the next afternoon, at a great Miami delicatessen. And so back to New York.

The next week I dropped in on Peter Stern backstage at the 46th Street Theater, and was immediately taken back in the *1776* cast. Later, we moved to the St. James Theater, then to the Majestic, and the show closed there in February 1972, after 35 months and 1,217 performances. It had been a great satisfaction to be in such an absorbing and lively chronicle of our nation's history, not to mention having many weeks' steady salary. The show's dialogue and lyrics are in a hardback book (Viking Press) and in it Peter Stone the author of the play describes the rare thrill of holding and reading the actual documents describing the birth of our nation.

It often happens that original Broadway cast members go on to repeat their roles in summer productions. And so in June 1972 William Daniels and Howard Da Silva again did John Adams and Benjamin Franklin, and I graduated from being a lowly understudy to play James Wilson of Pennsylvania. The Congress has decided that the vote on independence must be unanimous, and Wilson is ironically the man on whom the final vote depends. All the other colonies have voted in favor of it. "I'm sorry," he says to the conservative leader John Dickinson, one of the three Pennsylvania delegates, who has voted "Nay." "I don't want to be remembered. I don't want the responsibility. If I go with them, no one will ever remember the name of James Wilson. But if I vote with you [two out of three] I'll be the man who prevented American independence." And so the vote is unanimous.

The theaters we played that summer, The Municipal Opera in St. Louis and The Indianapolis Music Fair, were huge, and so our director Peter Stern had to make changes in the original Broadway blocking. Bill Daniels said he learned there that if you had a line of dialogue answering someone else half a block away on the huge stage, it was necessary to make some flamboyant gesture to direct the audience's eyes to you so they would see who was speaking. And then we had to re-do the blocking again, because our last venue, The Houston Music Theatre, a large tent, was theater in the round.

It was in 1973 that a summer package of *Annie Get Your Gun* was mounted starring Barbara Eden, known to TV audiences in *I Dream of Jeannie*. Auditioning for Jay Harnick the director and Marvin Gordon the choreographer (a neighbor of ours on Perry Street), I was signed to do Charlie Davenport, who produces the Wild West show starring Annie Oakley. It was what used to be called a bravura part, and I got some good notices for my "enthusiastic performance." We rehearsed in New York, of course, then played six theaters in the round (some tent and some hard-top) in New York, Pennsylvania and New Jersey.

Till then the show had been remembered principally for Ethel Merman's powerful performance on Broadway. Did Barbara Eden measure up to Merman? Of course not — no one could have, in my opinion. And her singing voice did not get universal raves from critics. But her glamour, her good looks, a good supporting cast and that marvelous Irving Berlin score gave the customers their money's worth. I couldn't help remembering having done the show at Tinker's Pond in 1963. Denise Lor, our Annie, had been pretty, perky and very outgoing to all of us, and full of charm and energy. Barbara Eden did not ever have much to say to the rest of the cast. There was a cast party at a hotel, but it was rather desultory. I think Miss Eden had been told it was customary to have one.

One of my pleasant memories of the tour was working with Alfred Hinckley, who played Chief Sitting Bull. Audiences and critics were fond of quoting his advice to Annie Oakley: *Never put money in show business.* I also remember Al Hinckley for his practical side. While the rest of us had to take all our meals at restaurants and coffee shops, he usually cooked his own outside the motel on a little charcoal burner — easy to fold up and put on the luggage rack of the bus.

In 1975 Evan Thompson was playing The Old Actor in *The Fantasticks* and asked me why I didn't audition for the play. It had been having a successful off-Broadway run since opening in 1960 and there were sometimes turnovers in the cast because of someone leaving for a better-paying job, or for other reasons. After auditioning for Tom Jones and Harvey Schmidt, I was given the role of The Girl's Father. *The Fantasticks* has become an American institution, and the few who have never seen it most likely know the songs *Soon*

It's Gonna Rain, Try To Remember and *Plant A Radish, Get A Radish* from the best-selling original cast record, which includes the original El Gayo, Jerry Orbach. *The New Yorker*, in its weekly précis of the show's plot, would sum it up by saying, "The whimsy is as thick as *that*." But, whimsy or not, *The Fantasticks* has been seen in so many places here and abroad, and heard in so many languages, that it is surely one of the biggest-ever American theater successes.

The Sullivan Street Playhouse was a speakeasy in the days of Prohibition. It seated less than 100. The floor was of tile, and in the basement were the actors' bathroom and the former meat lockers. The audience sat in four rows before the small stage, next to which was the orchestra, consisting of piano and harp, quite right for this intimate musical. It takes discipline and concentration to play to an audience most of whom are only ten feet away, but you as actors are not aware that it is discipline, so involved are you in *being* the character.

It was not too long a walk down Bleecker Street to Sullivan, and I was with *The Fantasticks* for a year — until the Andersons decided to leave on another trip to Europe. This we did in June 1976, taking Amy with us. We were able to do that because she had made so much progress since that awful diagnosis nine years before.

Autism, though it appears in so many different forms and degrees of severity, comes from the word *auto*, which means "self." Though some autistic people have surprising talents and abilities — we have all heard of so-called "autistic savants" — they all share one thing: the inability to easily communicate with others, and thus difficulty in living what we call normal lives. Amy's development had lagged behind that of other children her age. Her best functioning was in music; the opposite side of the brain from speech. There had probably been some brain damage during Alice's pregnancy.

From infancy she had been exposed to many kinds of music, including original cast records of Broadway shows, and pop music from the '30s and '40s, all of which she memorized and absorbed, better than we realized at the time. One cold wintry day when Alice was dressing Amy to go out, she said to her while adjusting heavy coat, scarf and gloves, "I don't know if you're going to be warm enough in this," expecting no answer. But the answer did come — in music. Amy hummed the lyric from an old record by Dick Powell:

Amy is ready for Halloween.

I've Got My Love to Keep Me Warm. She knew exactly what she wanted to say — and added a touch of humor.

In London we enjoyed double-decker busses and sightseeing. But apparently most important to Amy was that every morning there was a knock on our hotel room door. It was a waiter bearing a silver tray with our "continental breakfast" of tea and toast, which he placed on top of our TV. And as Amy went to sleep each night her mantra was *The man to bring the toast.* We did see one musical together, *Liza of Lambeth*, and Amy still loves to play the record. In Copenhagen, Tivoli Gardens was, of course, a must, and we celebrated her 11th birthday with my cousin Werner, who was now married, and had two little boys.

A great part of filmmaking for actors is waiting — waiting for technical problems to be solved, usually. What those problems are is usually a mystery to the actor, so unless you are a star and can relax in your dressing room, you just have to sit around and be patient, meanwhile expected to be fresh and brilliant when they finally get to your scene. My longest wait was in 1983, when I had a small part in *Cotton Club*, directed by Francis Ford Coppola. In the scene I was in, the head mobster is deciding what number to play in that day's game, and is getting inside info on what is getting the heaviest play. I was the bookkeeper, described in the script as *an ungangsterish gangster*, and come in and give him the info. I had exactly one line. The scene was being shot in a wooden two-story building on far West 59th Street. My call was 8:00 A.M. First, I was put in costume: sleeves rolled up, green eyeshade, and make-up — hair slicked down and parted in the middle — then told to wait. And wait. And wait. Very often I would bring a newspaper or a crossword puzzle to these jobs, but this time I had brought nothing. There was only conversation, and sitting. We were given food, of course, and a bathroom was available. The morning wore on, and the afternoon, then into the evening. Occasionally I'd think of the overtime we might get, but that was the only positive. Lest this story become as boring as the day was, cut to the chase. Believe it or not, we weren't called upstairs to shoot the scene until midnight.

The scene itself was very simple, and I was done in a few minutes. We were later told by The Screen Actors Guild that the company had gone bankrupt, but eventually we were paid. I made $900 in those wearisome 16 ½ hours, so I guess the boredom was worth it. I occasionally get small residual checks for *Cotton Club*, but have no way of knowing, unless the film is available somewhere, whether or not the *Ungangsterish gangster* is still in it. There is only one thing left to say: "That's showbiz."

In 1983 Juliet Taylor cast me in Woody Allen's *Zelig*, a brilliant parody of documentary films. I was one of the doctors trying to diagnose Leonard Zelig's strange malady, in which he takes on multiple personalities and appearances, depending on who he is with. Allen used several actual authorities to "confirm" and analyze the man's symptoms. And as I learned from him, comedy is serious business.

I was not an extra, nor was I a principal, and so I did not have to be paid a continuous fee when not working. The settings where I was used included what was supposed to be a psychiatric hospital in Alpine, New York, then Bellevue Hospital, also Columbia

University. I had no lines, but was seen many times conferring with the other doctors. Nor did I get any on-screen billing. In one scene I was seen injecting Zelig with a huge cattle syringe. In the closing credits *Syringe Doctor* was listed as being played by Howard Erskine, with whom I'd worked in Albany those many years ago. Days or weeks might go by before I was needed the next time, and according to my recollection the entire process lasted almost a year.

In the Allen films I was in (there were three) I was never given scripts, only pages of the scenes I was actually in, nor were any of the actors — certainly not those in smaller parts. Therefore, the overall film was a mystery until we saw it in the theater. I believe that was because Woody was continually working it out as he went, and the number of his outtakes has become legendary. This is not a criticism. It is just his way of working.

I had one line in the Allen film *Radio Days*, and that scene was cut. In *Hannah and Her Sisters*, I was a doctor trying to advise Woody regarding his sexual insufficiency. "Wouldn't it help to do pushups?" he asks. I had a nice little bit, but when I saw the film in its opening week the part had been re-shot with an actor 20 years younger.

Another time he had me do an on-camera audition for a part he was about to put in another picture. It was obvious he didn't think I was right for it. But, again, another lesson in acting. "Sometimes I prefer to use amateurs," he said, with words to the effect that the reason is they don't realize how important it is and so play it more naturally.

In April 1983 I was back at the beautiful Paper Mill Playhouse in Millburn, New Jersey, where I'd played in *Sunday In New York* in 1963 while courting Alice. I call it "beautiful" because there had been a fire there and the house, the stage and the dressing rooms were completely modernized, and it is now the equal of any Broadway theater.

The show was the classic 1928 Sigmund Romberg musical *The New Moon*, with book and lyrics by Oscar Hammerstein II. There was a complicated plot involving French aristocracy, political controversy in the New World, and villainy on the side. I was M. Beaunoir, father of the beautiful Marianne, Judith McCauley. Her hero Robert was Richard White, who, of course, she marries in the end.

I commuted to Millburn in our little Dodge Aries, and carried some of the chorus people as well. Many of Beaunoir's lines are remonstrating with his daughter. It was the stock role of the disapproving father, but a pleasure to be in a musical with such a beautiful score, of a kind which is not heard these days. It was a six-week engagement.

I have resolved not to bore the reader by listing everything I've done, but one minor engagement deserves a mention. It was one flight up in the old Diplomat Hotel, 43rd Street just west of 6th Avenue, where in 1983 and '84 Will Lieberson presented *The Quaigh Lunchtime Theater* — short plays done while people were literally eating their brown-bag lunches. The one I was in was *I'm Herbert* by Robert Anderson, and my scene partner was Fay Gold. There are two old people on the porch of a senior citizens' home, discussing their past lives, who they were married to (each other at one point), and various other involvements. As the play goes on they each get more confused, though, as to who it was, and when, and where. The play was concurrently hilarious, and a little sad. The sub-billing on the flyers was *Take Your Funny Bone to Lunch*.

An interesting film job, or series of them, was for Eastman Kodak. It was what is called an Infomercial for their products. I was The Professor of Light, and gave many basic lessons on how lenses work, and how light affects film. This led to several trips to Rochester, and I was always put up at The Strathallen, a lovely hotel in a park setting. At one point Kodak was introducing their new disc camera. Instead of a roll of film there were many negatives on one small disc. I had to sign a secrecy agreement — not a word about this new product to anyone. Ultimately the pictures on discs were not a success, and have long been forgotten. I'd commute to Rochester on fairly small planes, and since these jobs were all in winter the wings were sprayed before takeoff to prevent ice, which gave me a feeling of confidence and nervousness at the same time.

In 1983 we had been at dear old 87 Perry Street for almost 19 years, and were very friendly with our landlady Edna Nemy, a single lady who lived upstairs, and would sometimes entertain Amy by playing the record of *The Fantasticks*. She had had cancer for some time, and died in November. Her family, who were now the owners of the house, planned to sell it to settle her estate, and we were given notice to move. So it was now a case of where would we live. We looked at several places, all in Greenwich Village, of course, and were still considering them when I was called out of town in April 1984 to film a commercial for Household Finance.

The ad agency wanted a New England small-town Main Street look, and as the weather was still too wintry there chose Yorba Linda, California. I was Jenkins, in sweater and carrying a pipe, who said, "Somethin' special about small-town ways. How Bea fixes breakfast" — (strolling past the local luncheonette) . . ."Ahh — our financial district (pausing at Household Finance office). Miss that marble façade? Well, for my money matters I want what's inside. The Household Finance kind of attention. To give you the right answers — right away."

The feature article in the Yorba Linda newspaper related that the town hadn't had so much excitement since The Bank of America was robbed. The only negative note was that they misspelled my name *Author* Anderson, and I have been plagued by that all of my professional life.

The day after I returned Alice brought me to a seven-story brick building which had just become a co-op apartment house. It didn't have the charm of tree-lined Perry Street, but it was convenient to all transportation, important for getting to auditions, and was still within the boundaries of the Village. After being interviewed by the Board of Directors and arranging various legal details Alice and I moved in on September 1, 1984.

Amy, being resistant to any change, was given a *vacation* at her Aunt Margie and Uncle Charlie's in New Jersey while we moved, and when we brought her to our new home the place was still disorganized, but Amy's room was three times as large as her old one, and all her familiar belongings were neatly in place. There was one glitch. When we stopped the car outside the house she took off towards Perry Street. I ran and caught her and cajoled her into the new digs. Amy took a dim view of all of this. She sat on the bed in her new room with her back to us, for what seemed like a long time. Then she turned and we were met with . . . *a smile.*

Among our closest friends were, of course, Alice's parents in Linden, who we visited often. But just as important was my former Army buddy from Pocatello, Russ Jehn. Working for *The Hudson Dispatch* in Union City, New Jersey, Russ met the lady who eventually became his wife, Caye Bolte. When the Andersons became a threesome we often went to their house in Englewood Cliffs, just across the George Washington Bridge. We spent many holidays with them, and most important was always the music. Russ played his guitar, I brought the ukulele, and we found that we both knew dozens of the same old standards, which Amy quickly picked up. Russ had a PA system, and she delighted in singing into what she called his "muckaphone." Russ and Caye were Amy's unofficial aunt and uncle.

During this time Alice also realized her ambition to someday sing with a band — Russ' combo, "The Journeymen," which she did at two large charity social events. His sad death in 2004 meant the end of those days, but we are left with scores of joyful memories.

Another event in our personal lives took place in 1988. I had owned the cottage in Towners since 1949, but Alice and I were both beginning to have doubts about how long we should keep it. The drive to and from Towners was getting longer and a little more wearing, and so was raking a million leaves every spring, and other jobs of maintenance and repair. Our trips up there were seldom for more than a weekend, and in spite of the respite of the hill and the house, it was beginning to tell on my nerves and my body. And so in that summer we put the property up for sale.

We came to a compromise on price with a young couple named White, and the transaction took place in an attorney's officer in Mahopac on October 4, 1988 — still an important date to me, because it remains a reminder of how emotionally attached I had become to this half acre of house, rocks, trees, weeds, and peace.

On the last day I put Alice and Amy on the train at Brewster North, then drove back to the cottage to pick up a few things we would want to take to New York. After locking the back door to the basement I climbed up a little incline to the kitchen door, and was surprised to find myself choking back tears. The little house on the hill had indeed become as dear as a person.

About the time of the Andersons' big move from Perry Street two changes were taking place in the advertising business, which as an actor I was, of course, part of. For one thing, Madison Avenue was becoming less and less the center of the industry. Ad agencies were

A joy for 39 years.

tired of the very high rents, and wanted new buildings where they could have their communications built to order. A look at the telephone book told me what I had suspected: Young & Rubicam, at 285 Madison Avenue and 40th Street, is now about the only one that has not moved, merged with others, or disappeared. For instance, Dancer Fitzgerald Sample, my long-time Lucky Charms employer, is now part of Saatchi & Saatchi, a British firm, and is on the Lower West Side, at Hudson and Houston Streets.

The other change affecting actors is that advertising agencies have done away with casting directors. When they have a commercial to cast, they now call an independent casting director who is paid by the day, and only when needed. And so agents submit their clients to the casting director, not the ad agency. I was now very seldom going to midtown for auditions. Many of them took place in a 12-story building on West 19th Street, an easy walk from the Village, and casting people would rent studios there, with video cameras, and had boards prepared with the actors' lines written on them in large letters.

All of this became much less important in 1986. An agent I knew, Nita Smith, submitted me for what she thought was a shirt commercial. It turned out that information was wrong. It was not only shirts but a complete line of men's clothing. The Kuppenheimer Men's Clothing firm had in the early 20th century been an exclusive and expensive brand, started by Bernard Kuppenheimer of Chicago. Probably due to the Depression the firm went out of business. Meanwhile, Hart, Schaffner & Marx, also purveyors of expensive men's clothing, was looking to start a lower-priced line. The Kuppenheimer name had been bought by Sam Forman, who owned the Hercules Trouser Company, and in 1982 Hart, Schaffner & Marx bought the company and the Kuppenheimer name, and were now looking for a spokesman — a *Mister* Kuppenheimer, to personalize the business and give it a friendly feeling.

There were, of course, callbacks, and finally, I later found out, 300 actors had been auditioned, in New York, Chicago and Los Angeles, and in January 1985, *this was it.*

I had been visiting David Howard in Nashville, Tennessee, where he was now living, and where his wife Olive had been born. The three of us were having luncheon in their apartment when Alice called. "Get back to New York," she said. "You've got the part, and you have to take a physical before they'll sign the contract."

This was to be exclusive, which meant that I could not do on-camera spots for anyone else. The first year's pay was very pleasant, and before I finished being Mr. Kuppenheimer the salary would become quite a bit more.

There was some discussion at Partners & Shevack, the ad agency, as to whether Mr. Kuppenheimer, with that name, should have a German accent. Sensibly, that was nixed. He needed to have a first name, though. What about Arthur, I said. I am that already. Accepted. Then a morning session at a long conference table where eyeglasses were auditioned. He should look like a responsible middle-aged man, but not too conservative or stuffy. And his suits would, of course, be Kuppenheimer's top line, the Premier Edition. Before I was through being Mr. Kuppenheimer, I had more suits, jackets and neckties than I could use for the rest of my life. I would be driven in a limo to the airport, flown first class, and taken either

Mister Kuppenheimer.

to Atlanta, where the firm now had its own film studio, or to some other city where I would cut a red ribbon and preside at the opening of another new Kuppenheimer store.

The effect of all this on my family, especially Amy, was this: Previously, when I was out of town for theater jobs, she would mope around the apartment, and there would be a definite regression in her communication with her mother. But Kuppenheimer was different. My out-of-town trips were seldom more than three or four days, and Amy soon realized that when Daddy put on those special glasses it meant that he'd be gone just for a short while.

The Kuppenheimer advertising copy, and the copy for my commercials, was folksy and practical. "The $155 Kuppenheimer suit," I said. "You could pay more somewhere else. But why on earth would you do that?" We later recorded radio spots in New York emphasizing that we could sell for less because we had eliminated the middleman. The stores were modern, but not flashy, and the advertising logo was white lettering on a blue background.

Some of my more interesting Kuppenheimer appearances were in Atlanta — natural, because the firm's headquarters were now in Norcross, an Atlanta suburb. Another, in 1987, found me in Portland, Oregon, in period costume, in a coach pulled by a team of powerful black Percheron horses — part of the annual Portland Rose Festival parade.

Since Kuppenheimer customers thought I was the owner of the company, some of my appearances in the stores were in the nature of actor's improvisations — a role without a script. One woman asked me, "Are you really Mr. Kuppenheimer?"

"Is there really a Santa Claus?" I said.

Twice men came to me with Kuppenheimer suits which did not fit properly. I instantly took them to the store manager, who would see that they were altered on the spot. One older man accosted me in an Atlanta store. "You ain't no Kuppenheimer," he said. "I've had two of your suits in my closet for 20 years. You'd have to be about 90 years old." I explained to him that I was the *son* of the original Kuppenheimer.

I had an interesting experience during a day of shooting commercials in one of the Atlanta stores. I had a long walk toward the camera, which dollied back. They probably had a problem of the floor creaking, as with that "I Love New York" spot years before, so I had to be in stocking feet. I was to simultaneously walk normally, as if I had shoes on, hit the mark exactly so I'd not be out of focus, look natural and relaxed, and also remember my lines as I walked. There were several extras at the far end of the store, and my natural impulse was to say hello and have a little conversation, but I had so damn much on my mind that I didn't feel I could. Then I remembered Barbara Eden and her aloofness 15 years before and apologized to them for not engaging in small talk. After about three takes, the shot went beautifully.

The most ambitious, and no doubt most expensive, Kuppenheimer promotion was the Kuppenheimer Sports Council, organized in 1989. Several sports figures had already done commercials for us, with the theme of "I'm not Kuppenheimer, but I know a good value when I see one," or words to that effect. And the spot would finish with me saying "Well, I *am* Kuppenheimer, and I know he's right."

In February no less than 20 major sports figures, including Tommy LaSorda, Arthur Ashe, Sparky Anderson and Mickey Mantle, assembled in the Atlanta Women's Club to shoot a Kuppenheimer chorale, conducted by Mr. K., of course. We sang, to the tune of Beethoven's "Ode to Joy," "I'm not Kuppen, you're not Kuppen, he's not Kuppen, hei-mer . . . ," and after it I turned to the camera with my baton and said, "I haven't had this much fun in years."

One coda, not so much an ode to joy, was that after I had presided at the opening of a store in St. Louis I rented a car before returning home and drove to Springfield, Illinois. After visiting the courtroom where Abraham Lincoln had pled his first cases, I went to a nursing home there to visit Chubby Sherman, whom I had not seen for 20 years. Sad to say, he had no idea who I was.

My contract as Mr. Kuppenheimer coincided with that brand's high point. Sam Forman's plain pipe rack stores had numbered 41 when bought by Hartmarx, and the Kuppenheimer chain eventually grew to 200 stores in 26 cities.

By 1992, however, changes had begun to appear in the men's clothing business, due to a change in American habits — more casual clothes in offices, especially on Fridays. A headline in *The New York Times* read "The Power Suit Chills Out." Men were spending less and less on suits, and more on inexpensive sportswear, and Kuppenheimer began to close stores. Hartmarx, meanwhile, was concentrating more on manufacturing and less on retailing, and sold off its retail units, including Wallach's and F.R. Tripler. It held onto Kuppenheimer a bit longer, but eventually that went, too. So obviously there was no more need for a spokesman.

Goodbye to Mr. Kuppenheimer coincided with goodbye to Lucky the Leprechaun. They both happened in 1992, within weeks of each other. This was not catastrophic, though. Each gig, as they are now called, had been satisfying and fulfilling. I was now getting pensions from all three unions I belonged to, had Social Security, and other income as well, so for a decade had not felt pressured to make rounds looking for work. However, I was not disposed to sit around the house. What else remained in the future? I was sure that as long as my health held up, and it did, there was plenty.

15
CHAPTER
RE-ENTER ORSON WELLES

In 1983 I read that Orson Welles, having had an up-and-down career in Europe doing movies and other projects, was returning to the US to do the 1½ hour CBS Sunday television show *Omnibus*, of which Alistair Cooke was host, and directed by Peter Brooke. It was a most prestigious show, and a fitting part for Orson's return: the title role in Shakespeare's *King Lear*, with an all-star cast. It was now 46 years since I had worked with the Mercury Theatre, and I wanted to work with him once more. I was proud of the fact that I had always turned down background roles, but this time was glad to be able to be one of the extras in the cast.

Rehearsals were in a midtown ballroom. At the first break I went over to Orson, who was sitting on the edge of the stage, and said, "Hello, Orson. Do you remember me?"

"Please help me," he said. "I'm so tired."

"Arthur Anderson. I was your Lucius in *Julius Caesar.*"

"Of course, dear boy! How good to see you."

The next day was camera day, and I was told that I had now been promoted to a speaking part, that of First Knight. I remember that Mr. Brooke was rather cool to me, he having been preempted in this particular bit of casting. And there is no doubt that the actor who originally had the part cordially hated my guts. Someone gave me a video of the telecast, and though First Knight does not have much to say, Orson had once more been kind to The Boy Lucius.

One more contact with Orson resulted from a rather strange coincidence. In 1985, when I was Mr. Kuppenheimer, spokesman for Kuppenheimer Men's Clothiers, I was sent to Clearwater, Florida, to preside over the opening of another new store. I knew that living

Orson will always be a Presence.

there was my first cousin Edward Gottfredson, son of my late aunt Letitia, and this was my chance to meet him. Edward, a heavy-set man in his sixties, invited me to his house to also meet his wife Kathy and their sons Tom and John, and on the drive over he said, "I suppose you don't know that you are related to Orson Welles."

"*Hmmmmm?*"

The explanation was this:

My aunt Letitia Brookfield Macpherson had been abandoned by her husband Walter MacPherson, but he then occasionally showed up, apparently only long enough to beget more children. She now had four and no means of supporting them. They lived in Buffalo, N.Y. My cousin Cornelia was adopted by the Schaefers, a well-to-do family who lived in Oswego, while Ethel, being mentally handicapped, was in institutions for the rest of her life. Robert James, whom we called Jimmy, born in 1908, lived with his mother until she died many years later. Edward, the youngest, age five and born in 1915, was sent from an orphanage in Buffalo alone on the train to Kenosha, Wisconsin, a scary journey for a five-year-old I would have thought, but he told me it was an adventure. A kindly conductor helped him change trains in Chicago, and he was met at the Kenosha station by Mr. and Mrs. Jacob Rudolph Gottfredson, who had adopted him. Mr. Gottfredson was Richard Welles' half brother, meaning that they had the same mother, but not the same father.

Edward and Orson lived in the same town but not on the same block, and hardly ever saw each other. They did meet once more in 1930, however, after Orson's father Richard Welles had died on December 28. His young son was fifteen. Orson and his father had never had a close relationship, but Richard Welles had exacted a promise from the boy. He wanted to be buried at sea, he said, or cremated, but did not want to be put in the ground after he died, and young Orson promised his father that he would see to that. But Orson did not receive news of his father's death until funeral arrangements had already been made by his grandmother, Mrs. Mary Head Welles Gottfredson. The boy pleaded with the family to respect his father's wishes, but was not listened to.

My cousin Edward told me that Richard Welles' body was laid out in the living room, a common custom in those days, and a service was held there. There were flowers, and candles at each end of the coffin. I had read in Simon Callow's fascinating Welles biography, *The Road to Xanadu*, that young Orson would not attend his father's burial, and left the house in the middle of the service, saying that he had to catch a train to Chicago. I had always thought this was more than heartless and unfeeling until I found out the real reason: Orson was guilty that he had not been able to keep his promise to his father, and angry as well. Edward told me that on his way out of the house Orson remarked, "What a medieval display."

People on both sides of the Atlantic Ocean have continued to be fascinated by Orson Welles' creativity, and by the contradictory quirkinesses of his character. Like many actors, he had always been on the liberal side of politics, and once spoke at a rally for Franklin

Roosevelt who was running for his fourth term as President. They sat together on the dais, and there was tumultuous applause when each was introduced. The story goes that FDR turned to Orson and said, "Well, Orson, it looks like we are two of the most famous actors around."

It was on October 11, 1985 that I passed through O'Hare in Chicago to change planes after having shot a commercial in Iowa, and saw the headline on the newsstands: "ORSON WELLES DIES AT 70." What a tumultuous life, I thought, and what genius he had, and what a tragedy that it was never fully realized. I suppose that some day children will ask their parents, "Who was Orson Welles, anyway?"

But not in my lifetime.

16
CHAPTER
WINDING DOWN

After Mr. Kuppenheimer disappeared and my Lucky the Leprechaun was no longer prancing around, life slowed down a bit. The media, especially television, was not really interested in octogenarians. But this for me was a natural process. I found that I no longer enjoyed the thrill of a 6:00 AM wake-up call to go out of town on a commercial shoot, or an early flight to Indianapolis.

Anyway, in spite of graying hair and slower steps, I was still needed at home to share the responsibility of Amy. If things had been different, of course, we might all three have been touring with shows, or performing together, as our daughter was showing signs of being a ham, like the old man. As it was, ever since our Perry Street days, she had been enrolled at PS 226-M, a public school for autistic children, which was originally on 12th Street, within walking distance of 87 Perry. For several years she also went to special summer camp in Putnam County, until one July day when Alice was packing her camp duffle bag and Amy unpacked it and said, "No more camp."

Amy Violet Anderson has become more of a whole, functioning person than we ever dreamed she could be in those early years. She has been continually loved, led and taught, thanks to Alice's inexhaustible patience. In 1993 she moved to a residence in Riverdale, The Bronx, founded by one of our fellow parents at PS 226-M, and due to a creative and caring staff she and the nine others there are seldom without something to do. When they are not at their Monday-through-Friday day programs there are speech and body movement workouts, bowling, museums, trips to local shows and to a restaurant when somebody has a birthday — in short, much

The Three A's at Mohonk.

more than Alice and I could do for her. Amy does come to visit, though, be with us overnight, and play her beloved records and tapes.

In spite of fewer calls, I have still been able to express my urge to perform. In 1980 I began participating in the yearly conventions of Friends of Old Time Radio, a radio enthusiast's organization which recruits veterans like me, and we do recreations of the old shows. (Website: www.fotr.com.) The most obvious was *Let's Pretend*, and I have directed three of our broadcasts there with as many of the surviving Pretenders as possible. Another of my favorites has been *Fibber McGee and Molly*. I do a creditable Fibber, and the late Mary Diveny, a long-time friend of Alice's, was a great Molly.

Radio itself has become a different medium from the one in which I grew up and made a living. Once the focus of American living rooms, with its incredible variety of dramatic, comedy and musical shows, it has become a peripheral medium for news, sports and music, but the kind of shows I was in no longer exist. Recordings of these can be heard on satellite radio, and new ones are still done live on the BBC and the CBC in Canada, but there will not be any original scripts written or performed again in the US until sponsors can be lured back.

But every October some of us old hands stride, or maybe totter up to the microphones at The Holiday Inn North across from Newark International Airport and do our best to recreate those original shows.

Another channel for my performing reflex has been The Episcopal Actors' Guild, of which I have been a member since 1960. It is a charity whose members, some actors and some not, some Episcopal and some not, work together for other actors who, "between engagements" may need help with rent, union dues, or even a food bill.

Formed in 1923, the Guild's founders included Douglas Fairbanks, George Arliss and Mary Pickford. I was on its Council since 1965 and also edited our newsletter, *The EAGlet*. I have been in many performances in Guild Hall, and there are concerts and play-readings there as well. It is headquartered at The Church of the Transfiguration, on East 29th Street. Much smaller than The Actors' Fund of America, the Guild is more flexible in being able to help someone truly in need, sometimes with a check the same day. Membership is very reasonable (info@actorsguild.org).

Though I have not always been lucky enough to work with important theater companies, I have from time to time had the satisfaction of supporting some of them. First was in 1946, when Cheryl Crawford, Margaret Webster and Eva LeGallienne founded The American Repertory Theatre. They did nine creditable productions, ranging from *Henry VIII* to *Alice In Wonderland*, but the American Rep lasted less than three years. In 1997 I was able to endow a tile on the front patio of the New Globe Theater in London. Though I may never get there to see it, the Arthur Anderson tile is to me a satisfying reminder of my own theatrical heritage.

I think my most successful theater involvement was in 1963 when the Vivian Beaumont Theater was being built in Lincoln Center. You could contribute as little as a thousand dollars and your name would be put on a brass plate on the back of one of the seats. I didn't want name credit as much as identification as a member of the profession. When Alice, Amy and I saw a lovely performance of *South Pacific* there in December 2008, the theater had been remodeled, and I wondered if the brass plates were still there. Imagine my surprise and delight when I looked at the back of my own orchestra seat K311, and there it was: "AN ACTOR."

In February 1986 I had again visited David Howard in Nashville. He was very ill, dying from oral cancer, and gasped out a request that I be his literary executor. I promised that I would. In 1998, twelve years later, I was able to produce and direct a recording of six episodes of *Peter Absolute* that I had edited from the original scripts given me by his son, David Howard Jr. It starred Dick Beals, known as the voice of Speedy Alka Seltzer, and my cast included over twenty actors I had known from my years in radio.

Included with the recording is my booklet, *The Fabulous Erie*, the history of the Erie Canal and how it opened the first link between New York City and the western states. Started in 1823, the Erie was our first super highway. *Peter Absolute* was produced by Radio Spirits (www.radiospirits.com). Though David Howard never found the success he sought as a playwright, I have been able to preserve a colorful and delightful part of his legacy, and at least mark the tremendous influence he had on my life and my career. Another outgrowth of David's caring was my eighteen years on *Let's Pretend*, and from this grew my own project, the book *Let's Pretend and the Golden Age of Radio*.

My radio heritage also resurfaced in 1995. Sybil Trent had become a friend of Anne Meara. Anne told Sybil that she had been a devoted fan of *Let's Pretend* since childhood, and graciously consented to be host of a *Let's Pretend* Reunion at the Museum of TV and Radio (now The Paley Center), on October 31, which was taped and is in their archives.

The Museum has several theaters, and the crowd of loyal *Let's Pretend* fans, now middle-aged and older, gathered outside, forced them to open their largest one. The show had gone off the air in 1954, over 40 years before, but the store of happy memories remaining in so many from their childhoods was touching. It was to me also a tribute to the impact of radio itself, The Theatre of the Imagination, which to this day television cannot match.

In 1995, while on a trip to perform in Seattle for the Radio Enthusiasts of Puget Sound, Alice and I caught up with Kevin O'Morrison, that fresh-faced young Mercury Theatre juvenile from 1937, who remained a good friend. He told us that he had rocketed from summer stock and a role in *The Eve of St. Mark* on Broadway to the Army Air Force, and was in the cast of Moss Hart's *Winged Victory*. After his discharge he acted for two years in Hollywood films, then returned to New York to do *Charlie Wild, Private Eye* on TV and radio. His many television shows and voice-overs enabled him to support himself while he switched his profession to that of playwright in 1966.

The Morgan Yard, only his second play, is about an old woman whose family burial ground in Missouri has been expropriated by the US Army. It found great success, and Siobhan McKenna, who played the lead, won Ireland's Best Actress Award for her performance. Kevin's next play, *Ladyhouse Blues*, based on his family in St. Louis, was for two years the most performed play in America.

He continued playwriting after having moved to a suburb of Seattle with his wife Linda. He also had more success on camera, having played the doctor who amputated Robert Duvall's leg in *Lonesome Dove*, then being spokesman for not one but two RV manufacturers. Now over 90, Kevin has written at latest count three novels, two songs and 14 plays. His latest is *The Nightgatherers*, which, though unproduced so far, has already won The Pinter Review Gold Medal For Drama. It is about four men, ages 27 to 68, who live in an abandoned railway tunnel, which actually exists under New York's Waldorf Astoria Hotel. He, Linda, Alice and I continue to keep in touch, and he is our daughter Amy's godfather.

In my performing years I have been involved in many readings, showcases and off-Broadway productions, some of which were worth doing and some not. Of these one of my most satisfying was playing Polonius in Terry Schreiber's production of *Hamlet*.

Peter Fernandez, a fellow actor from *Let's Pretend* and now a film director, called me in 2001. He was directing The Cartoon Network's series *Courage the Cowardly Dog*. The dog belonged to the farmer Eustace and his wife Muriel. All sorts of bizarre disasters befell the family, from which the dog always saved them. He was never given credit for this, though, and the farmer continually yelled at him, "STUPID DOG!!!" The actor Lionel Wilson had been playing Eustace, but was now too ill to continue, and in May of that year I took over. I did nineteen episodes of *Courage* which are replayed in worldwide markets. It's fascinating; the variety of roles an actor is sometimes called upon to play, if he is as lucky as I have been. Here I was the innocent and good-natured leprechaun for all those years, and now I was being truly mean, bad-tempered and generally rotten.

There have been several enjoyable codas to my acting career. One has been that on every St. Patrick's Day I have received a call from some radio station wanting to interview me, and hear the voice of Lucky the Leprechaun, and they will usually have me do their station break as Lucky.

Another much more recent add-on was being called by Kevin Maher, an award-winning writer and director doing a featurette for Comedy Central which was shown on the Internet. It is a take-off on the Eleven O'Clock News called *Old People News* — "coming to you from the Quiet Room of the Sunshine Senior Center." I am the anchor, and my co-anchor is Lynne Rogers. We did several items presumably of interest to old codgers, and my closing was, "This is Charlie Mergler signing off. But stay tuned later for the Evening News, at 3:00 P.M."

Without going into acting theory (aren't you glad?) I will try to tell *how it feels* to be an actor. After getting the job and going into rehearsal there is always the insecurity of not knowing whether you're getting it right — if this is what the director wants — or if you ever will. But as rehearsals progress and the actors develop their relationships to the characters and to each other, and are up in their lines, there is a feeling of family. When you are rehearsing in the theater, you the cast *own* the place. You can lounge in the seats, as long as you don't miss a cue — think your own thoughts about your part, and whether you should have eaten that pastrami sandwich. But performing is another matter. Then you are responsible to the director and through him to the author, to the other actors, and ultimately to the audience. What a responsibility. And what a satisfaction — when it's going right.

Part of the wonder of performing is that when you are doing it in any medium, you *become* another person, and whatever is going on with Arthur Anderson, or whoever you are, does not exist. For years I was afflicted with nasty sinus headaches. I would sometimes have nausea, and Alice told me that my complexion would turn slightly green. I remember one matinee at Mt. Kisco when I was feeling particularly miserable. But when I was onstage doing the scene, the headache just *wasn't there*. It returned, of course, when I came off.

Thornton Wilder once wrote that theatre is the best way to learn what it is to be a human being. I have had that learning experience continuously since I was a child, from *Peter Absolute* to William Shakespeare (*Julius Caesar*) to Lucky the Leprechaun (though I admit leprechauns aren't *quite* human).

Though it may be fun to watch actors act, many people cannot imagine why you would want to *be one* — unless you have an insufferable ego, or are just too lazy to work at a real job. Here are opinions of two experienced actors: "Be a veterinarian," said Swoosie Kurtz. "I hate to be cynical, but I wouldn't advise anyone to go into this acting business." And then there is Mia Dillon, who said, "If you would be happy acting in the smallest theater, in the smallest town for no pay, then you belong in the theater." For myself all I know is, this is what I do, have always done, and never wished to do anything else — except when I was eight and wanted to be a trolley car motorman.

Also Written by Arthur Anderson

Peter Absolute on the Erie Canal
(1998 — Radio Spirits)

The Best Of Old-Time Radio Starring Orson Welles
(Radio Spirits — Foreword to companion booklet)

Let's Pretend and the Golden Age of Radio
(www.Bearmanormedia.com)

A Richmondtown Childhood
(Staten Island Historical Society)

Miss Cecyl and the Children's Playhouse
(Staten Island Historical Society)

INDEX

A

Abbott, George 181-182

Abe Lincoln in Illinois 99

Abraham & Straus (department store) 109

Abrahams, Nellie 15,121

Actors incorporate 162

Actors' Cues 90

Actors' Equity 36, 48, 92, 127

Actors' Fund, The 45

Actors' Studio, The 128

Adams, Mason 148

Adams, William P. (Uncle Bill) 64

Agents 95-96

Albany NY Playhouse 99, 107-108

Albee, Edward 134

Alberghetti, Anna Maria 139

Albert, Eddie 103

Albus, Joanna 120-121

Aldrich Family, The 63

Alfred Hitchcock Presents 48

Alice In Wonderland 205

Alland, William (*Vachtangov*) 45

Allen, Elizabeth 171

Allen, Woody 187

Allen's Alley 102

Ambrose Channel Lighthouse 8

American Academy of Dramatic Arts, The 136

American Dream 135

American Federation of Radio Artists 63-64

American Repertory Theatre 205-206

American School of The Air 49, 55, 57, 100

Andover NJ 137

American Theatre Wing Professional Training Program 98

American Youth Hostels 66, 70, 110

Andersen, Albert 5

Anderson, Amy Violet 162, 185-6, 202-3

Anderson, Captain 94

Anderson, Edward 8, 11, 17, 19

Anderson, George and Violet (illustr.) 17

Anderson, George Jr. 8, 11, 17, 19

Anderson, George Sr. 5, 7, 17, 157

Anderson, John 68
Anderson, Robert 189
Anderson, Violet E.B. 5, 11, 16, 17
Anne of Green Gables 48
Annie Get Your Gun 139, 184
Appel, Anna 67
Arliss, George 204
Army Specialized Training Program (ASTP) 77
Around We Go 120
Artists' Service 164
As The World Turns 167
Atkinson, Brooks 40
Atkinson, Brooks 40
Atlantic City NJ 73, 100
Atterbury, Malcolm and Ellen 107
Auditioning 33, 62, 96-97, 144-145, 164, 171, 179, 188, 193
Aunt Jenny's Real Life Stories 53, 57, 100
Auntie Mame 128, 129, 134
Auto-Lite Spark Plugs 102

B

Bacall, Lauren 171
Bain, Donald 32
Bambi 28-30
Barillet, Pierre 172
Barker, Brad 52
Barney, Jay 94
Barnum, Pete 30
Barr, Richard 47, 128, 134
Barrett, Edith 46
Barton, Barbara 107
Beals, Dick 205

Beckett, Samuel 135
Beggs, Malcolm Sr. and Jr. 13
Belasco, David 25
Bendix, William 133
Bennett, Constance 128
Bennett, Rudy 126
Bergen, Candace 161
Berry, John 48
Bertram, Bert and Rubee 161
Betty and Jean at the Twin Organs 13
Bevans, Phillippa 124, 126
Big Sister 47, 56, 71
Binns, Ed 104
Black Like Me 155
Blackstone Theater 174
Blackwell & Curtis 68
Blitzstein, Marc 34, 35
Bosley, Tom 141
Bova, Joe 162
Bowden, Charles 128-129
Boyd, Henry 100
Boyer, Charles 28
Brandon, Eunice 141
Breslin, Howard 102, 108
Brief Encounter 124
Broder, Jane 96
Brooke, Peter 198
Brookfield, Charles H.E. 114-117
Brookfield, Col. Arthur Montagu 5, 57, 114
Brookfield, Cornelia 113, 169
Brookfield, Edward 113, 160
Brookfield, Eugene 117-118
Brookfield, Jane Octavia 114
Brookfield, Violet E. 5

Brooklyn Academy of Music 110

Brother Rat 102

Broun, Heywood 37

Brown Maurice 64, 102

Brown, Chamberlain and Lyman 95

Brown, George Frame 15

Brown, Himan (Hi) 21, 23

Brown, John Mason 37

Brown, Katherine 27

Bruns, Phil 168

Buchman, Herman 98

Bucks County Playhouse 132-133, 170

Burke, Melville 68

Burrows, Abe 171-175

Burrows, James 174

Burrows-isms 173

C

Cactus Flower 171-176

Caine Mutiny Court Martial, The 133

Camp Anchorage 32, 50

Camp Crowder 80

Campbell (Soup) Playhouse 53

Campbell Soundstage, The 123

Cantor, Charlie 29

Captain Healy's Stamp Club 21

Car 54, Where Are You? 168

Charlie Wild, Private Eye 206

Carpenter, Francis 47

Cat On A Hot Tin Roof 104

CBC, Canada 204

Central City Opera House 172

Cereghetti, Peter 171, 177, 179

Chamlee, Mario 15

Chappell, Ernest 53

Chatterton, Ruth 20

Cherry Lane Theater 135

Chester, PA 77

Chicago, Illinois

Children's Playhouse, The 12, 13

Children's Program Waivers 63-64

Chorus Equity 136

Christmas Carol, A 14, 53, 54

Church of the Ascension, The 143

Church of the Transfiguration, The 204

Church, Sandra 127

Cinderella 3

Citizen Kane 45

Clio, MI 127

Coaxial cable 103

Coburn, Charles 126

Coca, Imogene 170

Coconut Grove Playhouse 127, 182

Colby, Ron 145

Cole, Alonzo Dean 62

Cole, Elizabeth 141

Collins, Ray 24, 45, 52

Columbia Broadcasting System (CBS) Network 22

Columbia Records 102

Comedy Theater 34

Composites 91-92

Conflicts 22

Copenhagen, Denmark 5

Copland, Aaron 33

Coronado, Benny 85

Cotten, Joseph 33, 35, 45

Cotton Club 187

Coulouris, George 37, 45

Countess Maritza 136

Courage, The Cowardly Dog 207

Coward, Noel 124

Cradle Will Rock, The 34, 42

Crawford, Cheryl 205

Crawford, Joan 139

Cream of Wheat 3, 64,102, 121

Cryer, David 139

Currier, Robert 127

D

Daddy Longlegs 20

Dancer-Fitzgerald-Sample (adv. Agency) 144

Daniels, Marc 99, 102

Daniels, William 183

Danton's Death 54

Danzig, Germany 7

DaSilva, Howard 181, 183

Date For Three 61

Davenport, Milia 39

David Harum 30

David Letterman Show, The 64

Davies, Gwen 3, 63

Dear Abigail 40

Dear Me, The Sky Is Falling 170

Dear Old Charlie 117

Death Dream 179

Death of a Dictator 37

Death Takes A Holiday 50

Dekker, Thomas 38

Devine, Jerry 100

Dietrich, Marlene 28

Dillon, Mia 208

Disassociate personality disorder 76

Doctor Faustus 47

Doctor's Dilemma, The 122-123

Dodsworth 67

Don Juan in Hell 45

Donald, Peter 20

Donovan, Warde 104

Douglas House, The 163

Douglass, Stephen 141

Downing, Robert (Bob) 104

Drake, Alfred 124

Drummond, Alice 135

Dunfee, Ethelynne 174

Durston, David 122

E

Eaglet, The 204

Ed Sulivan Theater 64

Eddy, Nelson 53

Eden, Barbara 184

Edinboro Road (Staten Island NY) 5, 7, 9

Edmonds, Louis 124

Eiffel Tower, The 113-114

Ellis, Mike 133

Elmer Gantry 67

Elton, Sir Charles (Bart.) 114

Endgame 135

Engel, Lehman 33

Entrikin, Knowles 66, 70, 101

Episcopal Actors' Guild, The 204

Equitable Life Assurance Co. 100

Equity Library Theatre (ELT) 97

Erie Canal,The 23, 24

Erskine, Howard 188

Essex, Harry 29

Eve of St. Mark, The 206

Exploring Manhattan 25-2

F

Fabulous Erie, The 205

Fairbanks, Douglas 204

Fantasticks, The 184-185

Farrell, Mary 107

Feen-A-Mint (laxative) 15

Fennelly, Parker 102

Fernandez, Peter 207

Ferris, Patricia 107

Feury, Peggy 128

Fibber McGee and Molly 204

Finish with a Future, The 127

Fishburn, Alan 51

Fisher Theater, Detroit MI 128

Fitzgerald, Geraldine 122

Five Kings 54

Fluffs (bloopers) 15, 24, 28-29

Flying Point Hotel, The 52, 67

Fooling Around in Ladies' Lingerie 110

46th Street Theater 179

Ford Television Theatre 102

Ford's Theater, Baltimore MD 68

Fort Dix NJ 73

Francis, Arlene 29

Francisco, Bill 158

French, Col. Marion O. 80

Friedman, Bruce Jay 177

Friends of Old-Time Radio 204

Frost, Alice 41

Fussell, Sarah 132

G

Gabel, Martin 41, 43, 47

Gag of The Month 93

Gallows Humor 135

Garden Of Allah, The 28

Gardenia, Vincent 135

Gart, John 102

Geezer, the 112

Ghost light 96

GI profanity 85-86

Gold in The Hills, or *The Dead Sister's Secret* 51

Golden Age of Radio, The 22

Golden, John 66, 89

Goldfish Bowl, The 29

Gone With The Draft 79

Gordon, Dorothy 55

Grand Central Palace 72

Grand Central Station 103

Grant, Lee 102

Gray, Sam 122

Greenhaus, Larry 63

Greenville TX 107

Grimes, Darryl 128

Grimes, Mrs. Cecyl 13

Grogan, Jane 117

Grubb Hotel 85

Guiding Light, The 167

Guild Newsreel Theatre 60

H

Hallmark Playhouse, The 16

Hambleton, T. Edward 122

Hamilton, Olive 5

Hamlet 207

Hammerstein, Arthur II 185
Hammond, Freeman 65, 158
Hancock, Don 102
Hands Across The Sea 124
Hanna, Art 98
Hannah and Her Sisters 188
Harris, Jed 60
Hart, Ellen 113
Hart, Moss 206
Harvey, Eleanor 108
Hatfield, Hurd 132
Hawaii 87
Hayden, Terese 92
Hayes, Helen 29-30
Haymarket Company, The 115
Hazel Flagg 126
Heart of Darkness 47
Heartbreak House 42, 49
Hecht, Ben 181
Heffernan, Johnny 8
Heifetz, Jascha 22
Heller, George 64
Hellman, Lillian 40
Henry Street Playhouse 33
Henry VIII 35
Hepting, Aimee 109
Herrman, Bernard 52
Herz, William (Bill) 45, 51, 52
Hicks, Melba 76
Hidden, France 126
Hiken, Gerald 135
Hilltop House 63
Hinckley, Alfred 184
Hippodrome Theater 61

Holland, Joseph 41, 48
Holmhurst Hotel 75
Hotel For Pets 122, 126
Hotel Paradiso 97
Houghton, Norris 122
House Un-American Affairs Committee 131
Houseman, John 34-35, 43
Hoving, Lucas 98
How Now, Dow Jones 48
How To Act In Motion Pictures 16
How to Get an Agent 95
Howard, David Belasco 24-25, 29, 34, 58, 64, 101 (illustr.) 193, 205
Howard, David Jr. 205
Howard, Sidney 108
Howdy Doody Show, The 148
Hughes, Ann 62
Hughes, Don 61-62
Humphrey, Vice-President Hubert 174
Hutchinson, Tom 24

I

I Dream of Jeanie 184
I Get Carried Away 126
I Love Lucy 99
I'm Herbert 189
I've Got My Love to Keep Me Warm 186
Indianapolis Music Fair IN 183
Informercials 189
Institute for Advanced Studies In Theatre (IASTA) 169-170
It Can't Happen Here 26, 67
Ives, Burl 104

J

Jack and the Beanstalk 3, 102
Jackie Gleason Show, The 168
Jackson, Anne 181
Jackson. Mary 124
James, Henry 115
Jehn, Russ 85, 190-191
Jenssen, Werner 160
John Drew Theater 158
John Golden Theater 69
Julius Caesar 34, 89
Jumbo 61
June Moon 98

K

Kane, Whitford 45
Kate Smith Hour, The 63
Kaufman, Bill 93
Kaufman, George S. 31-32, 170
Kaufman-Bedrick Drug Store 20
Keane 126
Kearns UT 81
Keene, NH Summer Theatre 64
Keep The Home Fires Burning 32
Kennebunkport Playhouse ME 127
Kennedy, Pres. John F. 48
Kennedy, Rev. Dr. James 141, 143
Kenny, Charles (Kay) 14
Kenny, Nick 14
Kilgallen, Eleanor 93
Kilpak, Bennett 23
King Lear 198
Kingsley, Charles 98
Kismet 166

Kiss Me Kate 141
Klein, Adelaide 29
Knickerbocker Holiday 104, 105
  (illustr.), 120, 122
Kremer, Ray 52
Kressen, Sam 133
Kronenberger, Lewis 68
Kuluva, Will 104, 122
Kuppenheimer Men's Clothiers 193-
  197, 198
Kuppenheimer Sports Council 196
Kurtz, Swoosie 208

L

Lady Next Door, The 31
Ladyhouse Blues 206
Lahr, Bert 129-131
Lakes Region Playhouse 127
Lakes Region, UK. 113
Lamour, Lt. 73
Lane, John 127
Lardner, Ring 98
Larson, John 84
Lawrence, Dorothy 19
Lawrence, William Hurd 19
Lawyer Tucker 101
Leasom 5
Lee, Dixie 108
Lenny, Jack 133
Lenrow, Bernard 132
Let's Pretend 3, 25, 28, 49, 53, 55, 56,
  cast (illustr.) 60, 61-64, 70, 89, 102
*Let's Pretend and the Golden Age of
  Radio* 63, 205
Levy, Estelle (see Gwen Davies)

Levy, Jessica 178

Lewis, Abby 155

Lewis, Sinclair 26, 67

Liberty, TX 130

Liebling, William 95

Liederkranz Club, The 56

Life and Legend of Wyatt Earp, The 175

Life With Father 47, 53

Lindsay, Howard 47

Little Dark Horse 68, 179

Little Girl Blue 61

Little Theater 55

Liza of Lambeth 186

Lloyd, Norman 47-48

Loew's State Theatre Bldg. 14

Loftus, Cecelia 68, 69

London Terrace 15

London, UK 112

Lonesome Dove 206

Lor, Denise 131, 184

Lou Grant 148

Loveton, John 58

Loy, Myrna 173

Lucky Charms, 144-154

Ludlum, Robert 141

Lumet, Sidney 122, 161

Lunt, Alfred 21

Lupino, Ida 175

Lyons, France 114

Lyons, Gene 102

Lyric Theater, The 50

M

Macbeth 89

Mack Truck Co. 17, 83, 157

Mack, Nila 25, 102, 121

Magnante, Charles 15

Maher, Kevin 207

Making the Rounds 3, 89

Mama 126

Mama, Look Sharp 181

Man Born To Live 113

Mangan, Buddy 33

Mantia, Charles 127

Mark Trail 62

Marlborough Blenheim Hotel 73

Marshall, Mort 164

Mary of Nijmeghen 70

Maxine Elliott Theater 47

Maya 34

Mc Fayden, Harry 58

McCann Erickson (adv. Agency) 157

McCarthy, Sen. Joseph 131

McCauley, Judith 188

McDowall, Roddy 97, 122

McGill, Earle 34, 57

McHugh, Frank 122

McKenna, Siobhan 206

McLerie, Allyn Ann 39, 158

Meara, Anne 3-4, 206

Meighan, James 29

Melting Pot, The 34

Mercury Theatre , The 33-54, 179

Mercury Theatre On The Air 45, 51, 52, 53

Meredith, Morley 104

Merman, Ethel 184

Merrick, David 171

Merry Widow, The 136

Meyer, Deed 149, 151-154

Middleton, Alice 134, 135-137

Midnight Cowboy 178

Mister Roberts 104

Mister Rogers' Neighborhood 176

Mockus, Tony 128

Moorhead, Agnes 45, 52

Morgan Yard, The 206

Mostel, Josh 178

Mount Monadnock, NH 65

Mother's Kisses, A 177

Mount Washington NH 124

Mr. Jolly's Hotel for Pets 122

Mrs. Brookfield and Her Circle 117

Mt. Kisco, Playhouse NY 208

Muir, Jean 158

Museum of Broadcasting, The 3

Music Box Theater 29

Music-Go-Round, The 126

My Sunken Living Room 123, 131, 135

My Fair Lady 158-159

N

National Theater, The 42

Native Son 45

Naughty Marietta 126

NcLerie, Allyn Ann 139, 158

Nelson, Barry 17

Networks – See NBC, CBS, NBC Blue

New Globe Theater 205

New Moon, The 188

New York Daily Mirror 14

New York Riding Academy 132

New Yorker, The 185

News of Youth 21, 23

Niantic, CT 56

Nichols, Ora 52

Nick Kenny's Radio Kindergarten 14

Nieporent, Andrew, Drew, Tracy 61

Night They Raided Minsky's, The 131

Night Walk 179

Nightgatherers, The 206

Nixon, Pres. Richard 180

No Time For Sergeants 127

Noa, Julian 24

Nolan, Jeanette 24

Norman, Craig & Kummel (adv. Agency) 134, 155

North Platte Canteen 81-82

Northland Playhouse, The 127, 158

Norwich, CT 106

O

O'Bradovitch, Bob 168

O'Brian, Hugh 171-175

O'Day, Junior (Michael) 23, 56

O'Neal, Patrick 141

O'Shaughnessy, John 124

Oakdale Music Theater 134

Oakes, Betty 104

Oh Dad, Poor Dad, Mama's Hung You In The Closet And I'm Feeling So Sad 135

Orbach, Jerry 185

Old People News 207

Olney Playhouse, MD 104

Omaha, NE 75

Omnibus 198

On The Town 126

Once Upon A Town 82
One Man's Family 121
Ostrow, Stuart 180, 181
Our Love Is Here To Stay 75
Our Town 10

P

P-47 fighter planes 83, 86-87
Pal Razor Blades 123
Paley Center, The 206
Paper Mill Playhouse,The 188
Paramount Theater 13
Park Central Hotel 23
Park Theater 13
Parker Playhouse, The 181
Parsonnet Films 94
Paul, Edgie 43
Pearl Harbor 72
Pemberton, Brock 89
Pendleton, Wyman 135
Pennsylvania Military College 77
Perner, Wally 132
Perry Mason 45
Peter Absolute 23-25, 33, 205, 208
Peters, Bernadette 177
Phil Silvers Show, The 167
Phillips, Lucille 95
Phoenix Theatre 122
Photo Modelling 165-167
Physical Training (PT) 78
Piano Concerto in B Flat Minor (Tchaikowsky) 52
Piazza, Ben 135
Pickens, Jane 124
Pickford, Mary 204

Picnic 124, 127
Pied Piper of Hamelin, The 13
Pioneers Of Television, The 163
Plant A Radish, Get a Radish 185
Players' Guide 92
Playhouse, The (Houston TX) 120
Pocatello Army Air Field ID 82-87
Pocono Playhouse 124
Poland Springs Hotel 139
Post Toasties 15
Powell, Dick 185
Powers, Tom 49
Pratt, Judson 167
Price, Vincent 29
Prince Who Learned Everything Out of Books, The 14
Princess Theater, The 82
Professional Children's School, The 20-21, 33, 48, 66, 109, 122
Public relations 84
Puss n' Boots Cat Food 102
Pygmalion 103

Q

Quaigh Lunchtime Theatre 189
Queen Who Couldn't Make Spice Nuts, The 70

R

Radio Days 188
Radio City Music Hall, The 48R
Radio Corporation of America (RCA), RCA Building 21
Radio Networks (See NBC, NBC Blue, CBS)

RADIO STATIONS

KSEI Pocatello ID 84

KXOX Sweetwater TX 87

WENR Chicago 59

WHN New York 14

WMAQ Chicago 59

WMCA New York 14

RADIO STUDIOS

NBC 21-22, 24

CBS 22

Rainbow Grill 30

Random Reminiscences 117

Rasely, George 98, 155

Ray Perkins Amateur Hour, The 15

RECORDING STUDIOS

CBS 155

Fine Sound 145

RCA 55, 132

Red Peppers 124

Redfield, William (Billy) 132

Rehearsal Club, The 20, 136

Reid, Elliott 48

Reid, Frances 133

Repeat broadcasts 30

Riano, Renie 133

Rich, Irene 30

Richards, Max 95

Richardson, Don 126

Rinso 70

Rip Van Winkle 13

Road to Xanadu, The 200

Roberts, Cledge 69

Robinson Crusoe Jr. 23

Robinson, Jean Greer 20

Roche, Viola 124

Rodgers, Richard 61

Roe, Raymond 69

Rogers, Lynne 207

Romanoff and Juliet 129, 175

Roosevelt, Pres. Franklin D. 201

Rootie Kazootie Show, The 131

Rose Marie 136

Rose, Billy 61

Ross Reports 91

Ross, John 62

Route 66 139-141

Royal Alexandra Theater, Toronto Canada 158

Rubinoff and His Magic Violin 22

Ruffner, Edmond (*Tiny*) 15

Rumpelstiltskin 3

Rye, Sussex (UK) 5

S

Saatchi & Saatchi (adv. Agency) 192

Saboteur 47

Sackett, Barney 127

Saks, Gene 177

Sandbox, The 135

Sanka Coffee 29

Savannah, GA 5, 7

Savory, Gerald 99, 103, 104

Schacht, Gustave 67

Schnabel, Stefan 40, 41

Schreiber, Terry 207

Schwartz, Mort 134

Scott, Raymond 29

Screen Actors' Guild 95, 187

Sears Roebuck 16

Second Hurricane 33-34, 63, 92

Selzer, Milton 104

Selznick International Pictures 27-28

Seymour, Dan 100

Seymour, John 155

Shaw, George Bernard 122

She Had To Go and Lose It at The Astor 110

Shepard, Joan 180

Sherlock Holmes 53

Sherman, Hiram (*Chubby*) 34, 41, 48-49, 196

Shirley, Alfred 52

Shoemakers' Holiday, The 38, 47

Showboat 126

Showbusiness 90

Shubert Theater 177

Shubert, Lee 34, 50

Shuberts, The 89

Shull, Leo 90

Shults, Mae 102

Siddown, John, Siddown, John 179

Silver, Fred 179

Silver, Joe 148

Silvers, Phil 167

Sinclair, Robert 158

Sleeping Beauty 3

Slezak, Walter 68

Smith, Nita 193

Sokoloff, Vladimir 54

Solid Gold Cadillac, The 170

Soon It's Gonna Rain 185

Sound Effects 30

Soundies 75

South Pacific 126, 208

Southampton LI Auto Museum 127

Spencer, Edith 100

Spruce, George 79, 121

St. Andrew's Church 11

St. Elsewhere 48

St. Patrick's Cathedral 23

St. Patrick's Catholic School 11, 16

Stadlen, Lewis J. 148

Stadlen, Peter 148

Stage Door Canteen 78

Staten Island Advance, The 13

Staten Island Savings Bank 16

Steel, Bob 57

Stern, Peter 179, 183

Stevenson, Robert Louis 52

Stewart, Paul 51, 56

Still Alarm, The 31, 60

Stiller, Jerry 3

Stone, Peter 183

Stony Creek Theater, The 45, 50, 64, 67

Stony Creek, CT 50

Stopak, Josef 15

Strudwick, Shepard 122

Subway Circuit, The 96

Sullivan Street Playhouse 185

Sunday In New York 137, 141, 188

Swift, Allen 147, 148

Switzerland 114

Sybil Elaine and Her Kiddie Revue 61

T

Talent Associates 93

Tamarack Tree, The 108

Taylor, Juliet 187

Teahouse of the August Moon 127

Teichman, Howard 701
Tennyson, Alfred Lord 115
Thackeray, William 115
Thaxter, Phyllis 65
Theatre of The Absurd 135
This Is Your FBI 100
Thomas, Michael 96
Thompson, Evan 180, 184
Thurber Carnival, A 97
Tiger At The Gates 132
Tinkers Pond Playhouse 139
Tom Sawyer 26-28
Tommy Knawker, The 173
Tony and Gus 15, 16, 21
Too Much Johnson 50, 51
Toscanini, Arturo 22
Town House 48
Towners, NY 109
Treasure Island 52
Tree, Herbert Beerbohm 97
Trent, Sybil 3, 61, 164
Truman, Pres. Harry 106
Try To Remember 185
Tucker, Madge 31
TV Studios 89
Twentieth Century 181
Twenty Thousand Leagues Under The Sea 132
Two Blind Mice 107
Two-Man Band 78

U – V
Under The Clock 115
Understudying 180
Union Pacific Railroad 81, 82

US War Bonds 84
Ustinov, Peter 129
Vallee, Rudy 126
Vanished Voices 23
Variety (magazine) 24, 90, 122, 127
Victoria Regina 29
Village Green, The 108
Village Voice, The 123
Vivian Beaumont Theater 205

W
Walgreen's Drug Store 90
Walker, Nancy 170-171
Wall Street Scene 34
Wallach, Eli 181, 183
War of The Worlds 53
Warburton, Charles 57-58
Warnow, Mark 29
Way Down East 30
Weill, Kurt 104
Welch's Grape Juice 30
Welles, Orson 33-49. 52, 95, 198-201
Welles, Virginia (illustr.) 46
Wells, Maurice 102
West Side Story 139
West Side Tennis Club 28
Westchester Playhouse 99, 103, 120
Westport Country Playhouse 158
What A Life 65, 67
Whipple, Sidney 40
White Devil, The 97
White, Onna 177
White, Richard 188
Whitmore, James 155

Wilder, Thornton 208
Williams, Tennessee 25
Wilson, Lionel 207
Wilson, Richard 51, 54
Windsor Theater 68
Winslow Boy, The 103
Witch's Tale, The 62
Wizard of Oz, The 126
Wolfe, Miriam 3, 62
Working actors 89
Worklight Theatre, The 40, 42
Works Progress Administration
  (WPA) 16

Wragge, Eddie 93
Wurlitzer's (store) 36
Wyatt, Eustace 52

X – Y – Z

Yellow Jack 108
You Can't Take It With You 126
Young & Rubicam (adv. agency) 29,
  61, 164, 192
Young, Harry 99, 107
Your Uncle Dudley 167
Zelig 187
Zoo Story, The 135

LaVergne, TN USA
18 June 2010
186656LV00004B/64/P